Ralf Fücks, Rainald Manthe (eds.)
Update Liberalism

X-Texts on Culture and Society

Editorial

The supposed "end of history" long ago revealed itself to be much more an end to certainties. More than ever, we are not only faced with the question of "Generation X". Beyond this kind of popular figures, academia is also challenged to make a contribution to a sophisticated analysis of the time. The series **X-TEXTS** takes on this task, and provides a forum for thinking *with and against time*. The essays gathered together here decipher our present moment, resisting simplifying formulas and oracles. They combine sensitive observations with incisive analysis, presenting both in a conveniently, readable form.

Ralf Fücks, Rainald Manthe (eds.)
Update Liberalism
Liberal Answers to the Challenges of Our Time

[transcript]

Zentrum
Liberale
Moderne

Bibliographic information published by the Deutsche Nationalbibliothek
The Deutsche Nationalbibliothek lists this publication in the Deutsche Nationalbibliografie; detailed bibliographic data are available in the Internet at http://dnb.d-nb.de

© 2023 transcript Verlag, Bielefeld

All rights reserved. No part of this book may be reprinted or reproduced or utilized in any form or by any electronic, mechanical, or other means, now known or hereafter invented, including photocopying and recording, or in any information storage or retrieval system, without permission in writing from the publisher.

Cover layout: Kordula Röckenhaus, Bielefeld
Proofread: Nila Sarabi, Berlin
Printed by: Majuskel Medienproduktion GmbH, Wetzlar
https://doi.org/10.14361/9783839469958
Print-ISBN: 978-3-8376-6995-4
PDF-ISBN: 978-3-8394-6995-8
EPUB-ISBN: 978-3-7328-6995-4
ISSN of series: 2364-6616
eISSN of series: 2747-3775

Printed on permanent acid-free text paper.

Contents

Update Liberalism. An Introduction
Ralf Fücks & Rainald Manthe 9

I Contemporary Liberalism of the 21st Century

Democracy without Freedom
Rainer Hank 19

Globalisation and Democratic Regression
Michael Zürn 23

The Revenge of Emotions
Karolina Wigura 29

Poison Cupboard or Treasure Chest? Why each Generation Needs its own Neoliberalism
Stefan Kolev 37

Do We Need a New Liberalism of Fear?
Amichai Magen 43

"Move Forward to the Back": The Illiberal Turn in East-Central Europe
Jacques Rupnik 51

Liberalism beyond Individualism and Capitalism
Christoph Möllers 59

Freedom and Justice in a Double Pack: A Short Journey through
the Liberal Intellectual History of Justice
Karen Horn 65

Ecology and Freedom
Ralf Fücks 73

II Liberal Answers to the Challenges of our Time

On the Critical Infrastructure of Liberal Democracy
Jan-Werner Müller 81

Freedom in Times of the Pandemic
Sabine A. Döring 87

Liberalism versus Right-Wing Populism
Sabine Leutheusser-Schnarrenberger 93

Ownership for All! From Class Society to Property Society
Ralf Fücks 99

Liberal Democracies versus Totalitarian Autocracies: European Responses
to the Systemic Conflict
Daniela Schwarzer 107

Global Migration and Cohesion of Diverse Societies
Cornelia Schu 115

Smart Market Design for Sustainable Infrastructures
Achim Wambach 121

The Future of Free Trade
Gabriel Felbermayr 129

I Tweet, therefore I am? For a New Ethics of Digitalisation
Alexandra Borchardt 135

Liberty Politics as Democracy Politics
Christopher Gohl 143

A Civil Right to Further Education
Ralf Fücks and Rainald Manthe 151

Authors 157

Update Liberalism. An Introduction

Ralf Fücks & Rainald Manthe

Democracy exists in fact only as liberal democracy. The chimera of "illiberal democracy" is only camouflage on the path to authoritarianism. In the history of ideas, liberalism as a broad political-philosophical stream of thought laid the foundations of modern democracy. It has promoted the separation of powers and the rule of law, the steady expansion of political participation and an active civil society. At its centre is the postulate of equal freedom for all and the normative idea of human rights. Both are subversive postulates vis-à-vis relationships in which they are not fulfilled. Even the concept of an international order governed by law is also based on liberal thinking. Liberalism has penetrated so deeply that we now use the terms "liberal democracy" and "democracy" almost interchangeably.

Liberal democracy is under threat

However, the success story of liberalism is not a guarantee for the future. Currently, liberal democracy is being heavily contested. Domestically, it is being threatened by populist parties and movements that attack it as a deformation of the "real" will of the people.

The populist challenge is far from over. Several populist candidates in neighbouring France competed for the highest office in the 2022 presidential elections. In the USA, too, the populist threat has not been averted. There, political and cultural polarisation has reached a level that hardly makes a return to democratic commonalities possible. In some eastern central European countries, parties are in power that undermine the rule of law, the independence of the media and the space for civil society organisations. In Germany, the right-wing AfD is gaining support in opinion polls and successfully competing for office on the local level. In parts of Eastern Germany, the AfD has managed to become the strongest political force.

Externally, liberal democracy is being challenged by increasingly assertive authoritarian powers, notably China and Russia. We are in the midst of a new ideological competition with authoritarian states. A new type of high-tech authoritarianism has emerged in China, combining totalitarian methods of rule with economic dynamism, technical innovation and digital surveillance.

As we write these lines, Russia is waging a war of aggression against Ukraine, the like of which Europe has not seen since World War II. Putin's campaign against an independent, democratic and European Ukraine is, at the same time, an attack on liberal democracy. The Kremlin fears nothing more than the spirit of freedom jumping over the border into Russia.

The flagrant breach of international law and the unbridled policy of violence of a permanent member of the UN Security Council mark a deep turning point. Putin's war has awakened liberal democracies. Germany is ramping up its defence spending and pulled out of its long-standing energy partnership with Russia. The European Community is moving closer together and the transatlantic alliance is being revived.

How can we strengthen democratic resilience, how can and should liberal democracies defend themselves against domestic and external enemies? This almost forgotten question can no longer be brushed aside. Freedom does not exist without a cost; it must be won and defended again and again. Ukraine is currently paying the highest price – partly because the West hesitated too long to oppose Putin's revanchism.

Challenges of the 2020s

But that's not all. The 2020s are becoming a decade of upheaval and transformation. Along with the new ideological conflict between democracy and authoritarianism, there are further fundamental challenges.

The greatest is probably *climate change*. It remains to be seen whether the destabilisation of the Earth's climate will lead to a kind of ecological emergency regime or whether a global effort will succeed in halting climate change through a new wave of green investment and innovations. A policy based primarily on restrictions and frugality will, at best, delay climate change, but threaten democracy.

The *digital revolution* affects all aspects of our lives. It is dramatically changing the world of work, such as public communications and the way in which policies are made. In the final analysis, AI and the progressive automation of complex activities lead us to question the dominance of humans over the machine world. Digital technologies have a great potential for freedom, but they can also turn into the opposite, as demonstrated by Chinese high-tech authoritarianism.

Western societies are becoming *more and more heterogeneous, socially as well as culturally*. This process is growing once again as a result of global migration. How can social cohesion and republican common ground be established in such diverse societies? How can we ensure equal rights and opportunities for all and avoid society disintegrating into identitarian, self-referential groups?

The Covid-19 pandemic was the precursor of a new type of global infectious diseases. It hit the world unprepared. In many countries, not just China with its zero-Covid strategy, drastic measures were taken in order to contain the pandemic. Individual freedoms were restricted in the interests of all. What can be done if the appeal for individual responsibility and solidarity is not enough? To what extent is the restriction of fundamental rights legitimate or even advisable in order to protect the lives and health of us all? Other dangers – such as growing resistance to antibiotics and associated new pandemics – are already knocking on the door.

Thus, the *role of the state* is changing. When things are falling apart, the state is called upon. It is taking centre stage again as a collective authority of emergency response. But therein lurks the danger of overestimation and overspending. Democratic resilience requires more than a state capable of action. It needs functioning markets and a committed civil society. This is becoming evident again in the great willingness to help with the accommodation of Ukrainian refugees. Market, state and civil society must work together to make liberal democracy fit for the future.

Liberalism under attack

It seems as if contemporary liberalism has little to say about these key challenges. That is another reason why it has often been on the defensive. It is often associated with market radicalism, egoism, social indifference and ecological ignorance by its opponents. Some critics accuse it of overstretching the claim to validity of liberal principles. Others suspect that liberalism has lost its emancipatory potential and has atrophied into the mere defence of privileges of the privileged. The insistence on individual freedom, the liberal independence from the state and the scepticism towards community utopias are now considered to be outdated.

We are convinced that liberalism as a mindset is not dead, but it needs a profound rejuvenation. This self-critical rejuvenation must agree upon the current conditions of freedom, and it must provide liberal answers to the challenges of our time.

What is the aim of this book?

Liberalism is a diverse and constantly changing school of thought. It extends far beyond the parties which include "liberal" or "freedom" in their name. There are free-thinking protagonists in all democratic parties and almost all social milieus. However, the conditions of freedom in the 21st century are different from in the early days of liberalism and different yet again from its heyday in 1989/90, the years of the end of the Cold War and the so-called "end of history". Liberalism must not leave the search for identity and common ground to the political right, social justice to the left and ecology to the Greens alone. It must find its own liberal answers to the great challenges of our time. The first part of our volume is all about this self-critical rejuvenation of liberalism.

The second part discusses liberal responses to the major problems of the 2020s: climate change, globalisation, the digital revolution, transnational migration. Which infrastructures do democracies need? How should liberals respond to the growing need for security and stability in a rapidly changing world? How must the relationship between state, market and individual civic responsibility be redefined?

After the positive echo on the German version, which was published in summer 2022, we decided to translate "Update Liberalism" into English to foster the international debate on liberal rejuvenation and liberal answers to the challenges of our time. We hope that the English edition will contribute to this overdue debate.

The texts

Our volume brings together authors from academia, politics, the media and civil society who see themselves as liberal in different ways. The fact that liberalism refers to different perspectives on the realisation of freedom also becomes clear from their contributions.

I Contemporary liberalism of the 21st century

Rainer Hank opposes a pure defence of democracy. Liberalism and democracy, he says, are not always the same thing. It is important to defend liberalism and thus *liberal* democracy. Now we have to fight for liberal tolerance and deal with opponents in a defensive way.

Michael Zürn examines the tension between globalisation and liberal democracy. The expectation that economic globalisation would promote the triumph of democracy has turned out to be an illusion. Instead, it has led to growing conflicts in the Western democracies and at the same time promoted the global rise of authoritarian populism.

Karolina Wigura pleads for giving more space to a "politics of feelings" again. While populist movements and parties mainly capitalise on the feeling of fear, liberals fail to make progressive politics with feelings.

"Neoliberalism" is an ambiguous term. It is often used as a reason for all evil against liberal thinking and politics. In his contribution, *Stefan Kolev* traces the history and meaning of this term and argues that liberalism must constantly renew itself, i.e. that new neoliberalisms are constantly needed.

A life of fear makes one unfree. Following Judith Shklar, *Amichai Magen* argues for a "liberalism of fear" that prevents fear from becoming the dominant mood.

Jacques Rupnik's text explores why a fertile ground for illiberal, authoritarian parties has developed in some countries of East-Central Europe. Demographic panic, weak liberal traditions, social discrepancies as well as a cultural definition of national identity form a specific mixture that favours national populist parties.

Christoph Möllers shows that individuality can only be understood as a social achievement. Freedom is linked to social conditions that have to be learned and preserved. This requires collective action as a medium of freedom. Modern liberalism must prove itself above all in situations where people are denied the freedom to shape their lives independently.

Freedom and justice are often traded as competing fundamental values in the public debate. In contrast, *Karen Horn* shows in her journey through the history of ideas that justice is a central concept for liberal thinkers.

Ecology and freedom also often appear as opposites. Especially now that climate change requires a drastic reduction of greenhouse gas emissions, calls for restrictions on freedom are growing louder. *Ralf Fücks*, on the other hand, argues for the innovative capacity of liberal democracy and market economy and outlines the potentials of an ecological modernity.

II Liberal answers to the challenges of our time

Democracy is built on its own infrastructures: parliaments, parties and independent, professional media. *Jan-Werner Müller* argues that the digital infrastructures of democracy – especially social media and software – should also be democratised more strongly so that they support the active participation of many.

The Covid pandemic was a test for liberalism. *Sabine Döring* considers a general obligation to vaccinate to discuss how freedom and the common good can be linked. In doing so, she ties in with Christoph Möllers: freedom only ever takes place in the context of a community.

Democracy must be defensible. *Sabine Leutheusser-Schnarrenberger* explains why liberalism must resolutely oppose right-wing populism. Liberals must find a way between radical individualism and false unanimity that denies social lines of conflict.

In another contribution, *Ralf Fücks* argues for "property for all" as the basis of a liberal civil society: home ownership and broad social participation in companies expand degrees of freedom and enable more economic co-determination.

Daniela Schwarzer analyses the new systemic competition between liberal democracies and authoritarian powers, above all China and Russia. She shows that democracies must be able to act both internally and externally and outlines possible responses at the EU level so that liberal democracies can hold their own.

Social approval of migration and integration is growing. How can we shape successful integration politically and strengthen social cohesion? *Cornelia Schu* gives five answers.

Achim Wambach shows that there are solutions beyond state ownership to organise important public infrastructures. With "smart market design", mobile phone or energy markets can be regulated in the interest of the common good.

Gabriel Felbermayr argues for more rather than less free trade. He also sees the dampeners caused by the Covid pandemic as only temporary. States should once again focus more on free trade within the framework of agreed rules of the game instead of erecting trade barriers that reduce prosperity and hamper innovation.

Alexandra Borchardt argues that digitalisation needs a renewed ethic. We must, she appeals, shape the digital world instead of letting it shape us. This is becoming a fundamental question of democracy.

Christopher Gohl advocates a new politics of democracy. For liberal democracy to remain adaptive and alive, democracy policy must find ways between technocratic elite rule and anti-institutional populism.

In the concluding article, *Ralf Fücks and Rainald Manthe* argue that people need a basic level of security in times of rapid change. Using the example of a basic education income that financially and institutionally secures a citizen's right to further education, we show how expanded individual degrees of freedom and coping with structural change can go together.

Acknowledgements

This volume would not have been possible without the support of many people and institutions. The first mention goes to the Friede Springer Foundation and the ZEIT Foundation Ebelin and Gerd Bucerius, which supported the German edition financially and have encouraged us to see that a rejuvenated liberalism is needed in order to continue to develop our democracy. We would like to sincerely thank Ute Schweitzer and Anna Hofmann, who have assisted the project with great appreciation and flexibility.

We also owe a great debt of thanks to our authors. They have responded to suggestions and have not complained about tight deadlines. Their ideas and texts sustain the book and enrich the debate. To contribute to the debate on a rejuvenated liberalism together with them is an honour and a pleasure for us.

At transcript Publishers, Linda Dümpelmann and Jakob Horstmann have consistently supported us, solved even difficult questions and contributed significantly to the fact that this volume could be published quickly. Last but not least, we would like to thank Nila Sarabi, Lara Schauland and Marius Drozdzewski, who have assisted the project at the Centre for Liberal Modernity and contributed to its success.

I Contemporary Liberalism of the 21st Century

Democracy without Freedom

Rainer Hank

Vladimir Putin's attack on Ukraine is often said to be an attack on the West. Therefore, "Western values" must now be defended, with the help of economic sanctions and, if necessary, with weapons.[1]

What are Western values? "Democracy", many say. But democracy has many varieties, and not all of them suit us. It is no more than a procedure for the legitimisation of a government by the people. The people can also elect scoundrels. That's not good, but it's still democracy. Viktor Orbán, the Hungarian head of government, is proud of his "illiberal democracy". Liberalism he hates, democracy he likes: the votes of the electorate stabilise his power. By democratic means and an electoral law that favours him, Orbán has transformed himself into an autocrat. His Fidesz party has once again won an absolute majority in the Hungarian parliament in 2022.

Liberalism and democracy are often used synonymously. This is wrong. When it comes to defending Western values, it should be about liberal values. They are the legacy of the (Western) European Enlightenment. I would defend liberalism tooth and nail. Whether I would always defend democracy depends. China and North Korea both have autocratic regimes called "people's" republics. When Indian Prime Minister Narendra Modi installs Hindu nationalism in his country, he has not betrayed democracy, but he has betrayed liberalism. When Poland's government replaces disagreeing judges and mutes the non-governmental press, it is not a violation of democracy, but a serious blow to the rule of law.

---

1   This article first appeared in the *Frankfurter Allgemeine Sonntagszeitung* on April 3, 2022. © All rights reserved. Frankfurter Allgemeine Zeitung GmbH, Frankfurt. Provided by the Frankfurter Allgemeine Archiv.

Are totalitarian systems doomed to fail?

One can go even further: liberalism keeps democratic governments in check against their susceptibility to be seduced by populism and nationalism. The separation of powers relativises the power of the executive and protects minorities against democratic majorities. For the American political scientist Francis Fukuyama, "classical liberalism" is an instrument "to manage tolerance peacefully in pluralistic societies". The central ideas are freedom, tolerance and respect for personal autonomy. These values must be guaranteed by a government that is in turn disciplined by and respects the law. The rule of law safeguards private property, freedom of contract and free markets: none of these may be thrown overboard by a democratically elected government. Liberalism without a market economy is not possible. Democracy without liberalism is possible. Whether liberalism works without democracy is debatable.

The fact that liberalism is in retreat everywhere cannot be overlooked. The American think-tank Freedom House subsumes only 20.3 per cent of the world's governments under "free" for the year 2020, such as Germany, France, the United States and South Africa. Some 41.3 per cent are "not free", including Russia, China and Venezuela. The remaining 38.4 per cent are "partly free", for example Ukraine, Hungary, Singapore and India.[2] Compared to 2005, the changes towards illiberalism are dramatic: at that time, 46 per cent of states counted as "free" and 31.1 per cent as "partly free".[3]

For Francis Fukuyama, these facts must be a deep grievance. In the summer of 1989, before the fall of the Berlin Wall, he became world famous with a single magazine article entitled "The End of History?"[4] Three years later it became a book; the title remained, only the question mark had disappeared. That was a bit premature, as we know today. Fukuyama's thesis at the time was that communism and fascism were no longer political alternatives, that the way was

---

2   Cf. Freedom House: "New Report: The global decline in democracy has accelerated", press release, March 3, 2022. https://freedomhouse.org/article/new-report-global-de cline-democracy-has-accelerated
3   See Freedom House: "Freedom in the World 2005. The annual survey of political rights & civil liberties", New York: Rowman & Littlefield Publishers, Inc 2005.
4   Fukuyama, Francis: "The End of History?", in: The National Interest No. 16 (1989), pp. 3–18.

clear for liberal democracy, an earthly paradise of freedom. Totalitarian systems were doomed to failure because they contradicted the basic liberal idea. That was a bit naïve even then, according to the motto good will prevail in the end.

Dispute for liberal tolerance

What is cheap, however, is the gloating that has poured down on Fukuyama since then. Nothing is more productive than an error of format. Fukuyama is still working on his misjudgement today. His latest book has just been published and is entitled *Liberalism and Its Discontents*.[5] It was completed before the outbreak of the Ukraine war, but has become even more explosive. The thesis, in brief, is that liberalism is not what it used to be either. Fukuyama expresses the suspicion that liberalism is partly to blame for the dwindling support for the values of freedom and the triumph of populists and autocrats.

How so? On the one hand, "dogmatic neoliberals" (economists such as Gary Becker or Milton Friedman) had turned the idea of free markets into a kind of absolute religion. They had not prevented crises of capitalism and had allowed the inequality of income and wealth to become indecent and unbearable in many countries. At the same time, the idea of tolerance and free speech had been ideologically deconstructed by the "left liberals" as a privilege to maintain the power of white men. The liberal mandate to endure ambiguity became a dogmatic identity politics, a distinction between friend and foe. In short, if liberalism itself no longer sets a good example, one need not be surprised that those in power everywhere turn away from it.

Fukuyama's theses are debatable. That makes them valuable. They also recognisably serve to legitimise the fact that world history has not listened to Fukuyama's thesis. I doubt that Putin, Orbán and Erdogan would embrace flawless liberalism if wealth inequality in America were lower and the LGBTQ movement less vocal. Despite its moral, philosophical and economic superiority, liberalism has always been decadent to its opponents; capitalism has always been denigrated by them as plutocratic.

For those who feel committed to the values of the Enlightenment, the only thing left to do is to fight even more resolutely for liberal tolerance in the fu-

---

5   Fukuyama, Francis: *Liberalism and Its Discontents*, London: Profile Books 2022.

ture – and to endure the aporia that there must be no tolerance towards those who base their politics on intolerance, war and destruction.

Globalisation and Democratic Regression

Michael Zürn

Globalisation has led to the temporary triumph of democracy. It foiled the socialist world's strategy of isolation from the dynamics of capitalist and democratic societies. It increased the pressure for renewal in these societies and ultimately brought them crashing. Without globalisation there would have been no 1989.[1]

At the same time, globalisation has brought forth and strengthened the new opponents of liberal democracy. On the one hand, through the export of capital and knowledge, it has introduced economic dynamism to regions that for a long time failed in the face of the challenges of catch-up development. East Asia in particular has benefited from globalisation and found its own path to prosperous modernity. Initially, this process could be observed in societies that also democratised in the course of their economic dynamism. After 1989, on the other hand, China in particular proved that there need not be a close connection between successful capitalist development and democracy. Globalisation thus also enabled the success story of an autocratic political system like China. Since the financial crisis at the latest, liberal democracy of Western provenance has been facing regulatory competition that, in contrast to real existing socialism, is both different and successful.

---

1   This short essay is based on a wide-ranging study published under the title "Die demokratische Regression. Die politischen Ursachen des autoritären Populismus" ("The Democratic Regression. The Political Causes of Authoritarian Populism"), Berlin: Suhrkamp Verlag 2021.

Globalisation has also brought forth the new opponents of liberal democracy

It is different because it explicitly does not link the flourishing of economic market dynamics to the institutions of liberal democracy and thus questions the seemingly inseparable connection between market and democracy. It is successful because the authoritarian ruling elites in countries like China and Singapore cannot be easily dismissed as selfish despots. Their policies have a recognisable common good component and can point to a track record of considerable progress, especially in the fight against poverty. They have also proven to be more successful in fighting the pandemic than Western European and North American countries. These states show that social progress is possible and this without the democratic control of those in power and the guarantee of individual rights, combined with far-reaching surveillance and reward systems. This undermines the notion advocated, especially after 1989, that liberal democracy has no alternatives. If China is seen as a regulatory alternative in parts of the Global South today, then the question of the right political order is back on the global agenda.

Rapid change has strengthened the opponents of liberal democracy

Globalisation has also strengthened the internal enemies of liberal democracy. Within the Western world, it has led to a dramatic increase in cultural diversity, to growing economic inequality and to the alienation of parts of the population from a political class perceived as aloof. These are the developments that have made the rise of populists possible. This refers to the parties and political movements that claim to give the ordinary people a voice again in the name of democracy, but at the same time represent a fundamental danger to liberal democracy. Indeed, contemporary populism is primarily an authoritarian populism. It is a political ideology that builds on a de-proceduralised form of majority representation and turns nationalistically against "liberal cosmopolitan elites". The topos "our nation first" expresses this nationalism. De-proceduralisation refers to the rejection of democratic argument about what is right. There is no need to negotiate what is right. It is set. "He knows what we want" was to be found on an election poster of the Austrian Freedom Party referring to H.C. Strache.

Authoritarian populist parties have a potential of about 20 percent of the vote in almost all liberal democracies in Western Europe. More importantly, a significant proportion of the world's population is governed by authoritarian populists. The best-known names are Recep Tayyip Erdoğan, Lech Kaczyński, Nicolás Maduro, Narendra Modi, Viktor Orbán, Vladimir Putin and, until recently, Jair Bolsonaro and Donald J. Trump. These are almost all large countries, which is what makes authoritarian populism so powerful for the international order. Authoritarian populism has spread globally in a relatively short period of time.

Authoritarian populism is widespread globally

Wherever authoritarian populists have come to power, we are experiencing a democratic backsliding. In all eight countries mentioned (Brazil, Turkey, Poland, Venezuela, India, Hungary, Russia and the USA), the Gothenburg Democracy Barometer VDem shows a clear deterioration in the quality of democracy. At the same time, the quality of democratic governance has worsened even in supposedly consolidated democracies. If the decline of democracy was for a long time regarded as something that only took place in distant countries, from the perspective of Western Europeans, the strikes are now getting closer. Not only in Venezuela or Brazil, but also in the USA and Poland, democracy has deteriorated significantly over the past decade. In some of these countries, there is hope that a change of government will reverse the trend; but where liberal democracy has already been replaced by an electoral autocracy, voting out the government is also becoming increasingly less likely.

Changes in the functioning of democracy are crucial for the widespread alienation from democracy. The discussion so far has focused strongly on the economic and cultural causes of authoritarian populism. While growing inequality in rich countries certainly plays a role and a cultural backlash may be observed to some extent, the political question is the actual key. Economic and also cultural explanations assume that people are dissatisfied with specific policies and therefore turn to authoritarian populist parties. Surveys show, however, that the dissatisfaction is mostly based on a systemic criticism of the political class and the established mainstream parties. Economic satisfaction, on the other hand, is relatively high and gender equality policies enjoy broad support.

People no longer feel noticed in a democracy

The political explanation says that it is dissatisfaction with the political system that is instrumentalised by the authoritarian populists for their purposes. On the one hand, many people do not feel adequately represented by their parliaments. MPs are perceived as a professionalised political class that operates in a bubble, detached from the interests of voters. On the other hand, over the past three decades, decision-making powers have been shifted to a considerable extent from majority institutions (MIs), such as parties and parliaments, to non-majority institutions (NMIs), such as central banks, constitutional courts, and international institutions. Decisions are made increasingly by institutions that are not subject to the majority principle, nor to the accountability obligations of representative bodies. The purpose of many NMIs is to enforce the triple liberalism of individual rights, international rules, and open markets.

Against the backdrop of these two mechanisms, many people obviously have the impression that they have been left out of politics – and this perception has a real basis. Not all groups have the same chance of having their concerns heard and implemented politically. This has allowed the idea to spread that there is a homogeneous political class that does its thing aloof from the population, serving the interests of a pampered and potentially corrupt cosmopolitan class. Accordingly, most authoritarian-populist campaigns do not seem to criticise concrete economic or cultural policies, but the system that produces them, i.e., the "parties of the system", the "left-red-green infested system" and the entire political class, and above all, the declared enemy, Angela Merkel.

The current retreat of democracy seems to be more than a temporary phenomenon. The optimistic narrative according to which democracy spreads in waves with only short periods of partial regression between them hardly coincides with the actual development. Rather, in retrospect, the period from 1945 to the end of the 20th century in particular proved to be a phase of worldwide democratisation. However, that half century was characterised by a positive environment that do not exist in the same way today. The democratic progression was not so much the result of an inevitable logic of progress, but rather owed to a specific historical constellation. The change in these specific circumstances now makes democratic regression possible. Societies do not slide towards liberal democracy on a predefined trajectory, but rather evolve through political conflicts and struggles for the expansion of social and democratic rights – and these conflicts can not only slow down the journey, but also lead to a change in the station of destination.

A new brand of liberalism must first and foremost reconcile

A new brand of liberalism must reconcile cosmopolitanism and democracy institutionally in order to get back on the right track. Real changes in our democracy are required to counter the success of the authoritarian populists. Looking exclusively at the characteristics and strategies of the opponents only leads to the reproduction of friend-foe thinking. It deprives us of the insight into the central questions we have to ask ourselves in order to deprive authoritarian populism of its basis: How can we solve the problem of representation? How can we reform non-majoritarian institutions so that they become more responsive and continue to deliver good outcomes in a complex, globalised, and pluralised world? Simplistic solutions that aim to re-nationalise and homogenise the institutional foundations of democracy, as demanded by authoritarian populists, fall short in a globalised world. So, what to do? The answer of a new brand of liberalism must be to venture more democracy and promote tolerance of complexity in our society.

The Revenge of Emotions

Karolina Wigura

Amid the rapid turmoil brought about by the coronavirus pandemic, it has become increasingly clear how great a role emotions play in global politics. Emotions influenced the decisions of entire states to introduce strict lockdown conditions. They also underpin the great protest movements we have observed throughout 2020. From Black Lives Matter demonstrations in the US and UK through protests in defence of women's rights in Poland, those phenomena have their source in a great intensification of social emotions during the pandemic. Fear and anxiety easily change into anger and rage which has been illustrated well by those movements of protest.

One might wonder what's so strange about this. For centuries people have been aware that politics appeals to emotions. Leaders of various greater and lesser states have perfected their ability to spark emotions among their subjects at least since the days of Machiavelli, who, in his famous treatise *The Prince*, claimed that a ruler should be able to effectively strike both fear and love.[1]

Today, however, in the era of social media, emotions are not just an accessory to political strategy. They're at its very heart, and those who can make the best use of them are also effective at winning elections. This is especially challenging for those politicians who wish to defend liberal democracy. After all, in recent years it has been its enemies who, for various reasons, have perfected the art of addressing mass emotions. The French philosopher Pierre Hassner wrote a few years ago about what he called the "revenge of the passions."[2] We truly live in the times of the revenge of emotion. This calls for understanding and an appropriate reaction.

---

1   See Machiavelli, Niccolò: Der Fürst, Stuttgart: Kröner Verlag 1978.
2   Hassner, Pierre: Rache der Leidenschaften: Metamorphosen von Gewalt und politischen Krisen, Paris: Fayard 2015.

Is politics the domain of reason or passion?

Until recently politics appeared to be a domain of reason. Since liberal democracy defeated fascism in 1945, the belief has been that emotions in politics lead to bloody upheavals and ethnic cleansing. That they should be treated with suspicion. And that good political systems should first and foremost promote education, law, constitutionalism and independent institutions. Additionally, the idea was to gradually increase standards of living so that people never again experienced the level of anger and frustration that once led to the dominance of political extremes and cruelty previously unprecedented in Europe. This was to guarantee that order and stability would be more durable than ever before.

A few years ago, however, things began to change. All at once, citizens of many countries began to express anxiety, frustration, fear and anger. They addressed these emotions against the liberal elites that governed them. Then there were also politicians who readily seized on this public mood: the illiberals. Unlike their liberal counterparts, they expressed an understanding for these emotions. They provided a vent for these feelings and directed them against the old political and legal elites, foreign migrants and people living in a different way than the majority. As a remedy, the illiberals promised a new wave of democratization, supposedly placing public institutions in the hands of citizens.

An example of exactly this kind of phenomenon is the victory and continuing popularity of Poland's Law and Justice party (PiS) with its anti-elitist, anti-minority and anti-liberal rhetoric. But PiS is certainly not unique. A long list of groups around the globe are cut from a similar cloth and they are either winning elections or gaining sizeable support. The list includes Donald Trump in the USA, Alternative für Deutschland in Germany, Thierry Baudet's Forum for Democracy in the Netherlands, Brexit supporters in the UK, Fidesz in Hungary, and so forth.

Electoral victories by these politicians rapidly result in either the decomposition of the rule of law and independent institutions (as is the case in Poland) or at least put massive pressure on them (like in the USA). At the same time they enjoy social support. In Poland, PiS is in power for a second parliamentary term and has also had its president re-elected. In Hungary, Victor Orbán wins elections one after another. When observing what is happening, liberals often reproach citizens by claiming they have been bought by illiberals, that their resentment and cynicism have allowed these changes to take place.

Democracy and a sense of loss

All this can also be described differently. The reasons behind the current political situation, and also the key to moving past it, lie in the great social and cultural shift in mass emotions we are all subject to.

"Step-by-step, year-by-year, the world is improving. Not on every single measure every single year, but as a rule. Though the world faces huge challenges, we have made tremendous progress. This is the fact-based worldview."[3] This is how, in his beautiful book *Factfulness*, the Swedish doctor and researcher on public health Hans Rosling describes the effects of the progress that has occurred globally in recent history.

These changes span the last 200 years, but their greatest acceleration has fallen in the last half a century. In particular, these include the reduction in infant mortality rates; higher life expectancy; access to running water in households; an enhanced level of education for boys and girls; dietary standards; access to technological developments such as cars, computers and mobile phones; and, above all, an increase in the level of wealth of entire societies, raising them from the lowest to at least average levels of affluence.

It would seem that this great scientific and technological shift and the transformation in ways of life should lead to increased optimism for the future and to a belief that we and our children can expect to live in a better world. Yet the paradox is that by reaching collective success, we feel deeply frustrated. Why is that so?

Like any change, development also comes at a cost. This is because change means loss. Longstanding ties, cemented by tradition and social order, fall apart. Behavioral strategies, which thus far have functioned perfectly, lose their effectiveness. A loss of tried and tested habits occurs. And so, development is difficult for emotional reasons; not despite the fact that it brings success, but precisely because it does. This leads to the experience of a powerful emotion, namely a sense of loss. From there, we are just a step away from fear, frustration and anxiety.

The politicians who were first to understand this mechanism have been able to perform great feats in recent years. The perfect illustration of this phenomenon is the success of Jarosław Kaczyński's political group in Poland. He was able to translate the rather ambivalent and undefined sense of loss

---

3   Rosling, Hans: Factfulness. Wie wir lernen die Welt so zu sehen, wie sie wirklich ist, Berlin: Ullstein Taschenbuch Verlag 2019.

into very concrete emotions: the fear of migrants and minority groups (like the LGBT community), anger with the liberal elites, with the founding fathers and mothers of the Third Polish Republic.

We could find a similar explanation for the success enjoyed by the Alternative für Deutschland. Again, the situation could easily be misunderstood. Many people in my country, like in other post-communist states, believe eastern Germany should be bubbling with enthusiasm related to its transformation after 1989. When the wall came down and international powers permitted the re-unification of Germany, the GDR was the only former post-communist state that did not need to worry about where to find the funds for its modernization. West Germany pumped exorbitant amounts of money into the infrastructure of the eastern Länder. Train stations and roads were either refurbished or built anew, and historic cities were rebuilt. It was assumed that the transformation would happen quickly, almost like a second Marshall Plan.

However, it quickly turned out that, contrary to initial expectations, the former GDR has not repeated the economic miracle of West Germany under Chancellor Erhard. Key macroeconomic values (a lower rate of economic growth, a surge in unemployment, etc.) were markedly different to those of 1950s West Germany. It is, then, no wonder that even though Germany has been celebrating the 30-year anniversary of its unification, the German media is full of skepticism and doubt about the real consequences of the reunification process. Discussions point to shortcomings, lost chances for entire groups of the population, unequal pay. Another argument, raised in the discussions about 30th Anniversary of German unification is the missing recognition of easter German achievements after 1989. There are also nearly no elites from eastern Germany. The political beneficiary of all these reservations in the eastern Länder is none other than Alternative für Deutschland.

Empathy, belonging, and pluralism

So, what should the defenders of liberal democracy do in the current situation? For many, the first intuitive response to politics red-hot with emotion is that of reason. And there are good grounds for it. The history of European politics of at least this past century has taught us to be cautious when it comes to this sphere of the individual and social *psyche*. It is easy to manipulate emotions, recent examples of which include both the atrocities caused by national socialism in Germany and all sorts of other nationalists, for example those whose actions led to war in the former Yugoslavia.

And so, the intellectual fathers and mothers of modern liberal democracy, like the popular German philosopher Jürgen Habermas or the American thinker Martha Nussbaum, encourage us to approach emotions with caution, and to transform them into ideas, or at least into careful liberal education. In the view of Habermas, a new kind of patriotism should be invented: instead of national feelings which may at times transform into exclusion of whole social groups and hostility, the philosopher proposes the concept of constitutional patriotism, based on the Basic Law in Germany and the Lisbon Treaty for the EU.[4]

Nussbaum, on the other hand, has given a lot of reflection to love, fear, and other emotions crucial to our collective lives.[5] When it comes to dealing with emotions in politics, however, what she suggests is a rather utopian project of "Socratic pedagogy" which is to lead to critical understanding first and only then to compassion and sympathy. This approach is informed by the fact that many people who comprehend the cost of transformation and the sense of loss would be more likely to say that it is much better to focus on the rule of law, and institutions, rather than the unpredictable reactions of the heart.

But there is also another way of approaching emotions in politics. Instead of removing them, we should look for such ways of working with them, and for such language of expressing them, that would make them serve a better, not worse, political community. At the same time, this should allow for effectiveness at the ballot box. An innovation in liberal politics, therefore, is a return to the sense of loss and an attempt to have a conversation with that emotion, an attempt to respond to it with empathy and to create an alternative to illiberal projects – in the form of an unxenophobic sense of belonging to one's own political community.

The collective sense of loss I have described can be likened to grief after the loss of a loved one. In the process of grieving, our first reaction is to look back and to dwell on the loss. And so, we could compare the content of reactionary illiberalism to precisely this phase of grieving. Yet from the experience we have as people, we know that grieving also has other phases. One of them is the one during which we work on reviving ourselves and on the sources of hope for the

---

4 Habermas, Jürgen: Eine Art Schadensabwicklung, Berlin: Suhrkamp 1987.
5 Nussbaum, Martha: Königreich der Angst. Gedanken zur aktuellen politischen Krise, München: btb 2020.

future. This is the phase that requires courage, hope and compassion, especially for those who are unlike us.

This, then, could shape the future direction of liberalism. This sort of political project has already begun to sprout internationally. Zuzana Čaputová's landslide victory in the 2019 presidential elections in Slovakia could be explained through her positioning of empathy at the very heart of her campaign. The previously little-known activist won the 2019 presidential race with a commanding 58 % of the vote in Slovakia, long dominated by the populist party Smer-SD (Direction–Social Democracy). In my country, Poland, the mayoral candidate Rafał Trzaskowski crushed a rival from PiS in the first round in Warsaw's 2018 municipal election. Even if Trzaskowski lost the 2020 presidential election, the sheer scale of support for him showed that making empathy an important, or even essential element of political language, is key to success at the polls.

Emotions and Covid-19 pandemic

To conclude, we should return to the Covid-19 pandemic, to the question of its impact on collective emotions and of how politicians can react to them. When the pandemic broke, historic accounts of various epidemics in the history of our continent (and, more broadly, the entire planet) were helpful in suggesting what emotions would be stirred up, and what role they could play. The first and most important emotion tied to a pandemic is, of course, fear. This fear has many possible facets, but our reactions to it have remained unchanged for centuries. Today, just as in Boccacio's day, we hear of the fear people have of a dangerous illness, spread around by those who live among us, by our own neighbors.

The second emotion widely spoken about since the great epidemics of ancient Europe is suspiciousness. In his *History of the Peloponnesian War*, Thucydides recounts the suspicion that the disease was created by Peloponnesians, who allegedly poisoned the water in wells.[6] 14th century documents recount how Jewish pogroms were caused by the suspicion that Jews harbored the Black Death. How is all this different to today's gossip that the coronavirus is the product of a Chinese, or even Chinese-Jewish conspiracy?

---

6   Thukydides: Geschichte des peloponnesischen Krieges, Leipzig: Reclam 2000.

Finally, the third basic pandemic emotion is uncertainty. This emotion is also widely discussed in historic accounts of epidemics. Uncertainty was predominantly linked to the fact that the rule of law crumbled under plagues – it was no longer clear what common rules were in place anymore.

The current pandemic and its concomitant emotions create an additional film over all that that had previously functioned in global politics. If the opponents of populists really dream of taking power from them, or at least of diminishing their popularity, they will have to consider all that is currently at play. Joe Biden and Kamala Harris, after the victory in the US presidential election, did not hesitate to appeal to courage and hope for the future. This might be the first sign of liberals being ready to reinvent politics for the XXI century, translating fear into courage, suspiciousness into caution and uncertainty into creativity.

Poison Cupboard or Treasure Chest? Why each Generation Needs its own Neoliberalism

Stefan Kolev

It's strange: For some time, neoliberalism has been blamed for all kinds of wickedness. At the same time, the author of this essay likes to call himself a neoliberal and, indeed, believes that he is not an evil person. How does this fit together?

Like many contested notions, neoliberalism has a complicated history, with various protagonists pursuing their agendas, leaving behind tracks that are not always easy to retrace. Nevertheless, the journey is worthwhile, especially for liberals. For, as will be pointed out in this essay, there is also a interpretation of neoliberalism that could be of significance for the future of liberalism.

The laborious unravelling of a confusion of terms

In literature, a distinction is usually made between two meanings: neoliberalism in the 1930s and 1940s and neoliberalism since the 1970s. The former was a self-designation by liberals, the latter is an external appellation attributed by often illiberal authors to various phenomena. However, they can hardly be more different in terms of content. While the neoliberals of the 1930s and 1940s sought to conceptualise a new, humanist liberalism for the 20th century, nowadays, everything which aims to dehumanise economy and society is termed neoliberal. How did this come about?

The 1930s and 1940s were the darkest times for freedom in the modern age. When a last cohort of liberal thinkers met at the Walter Lippmann Colloquium in Paris in 1938, it was not easy to believe in the future of the liberal order.[1]

---

1 Cf. Reinhoudt, Jurgen/Audier, Serge: The Walter Lippmann Colloquium: The Birth of Neo-Liberalism, London: Palgrave Macmillan 2018.

At the conference, which was dedicated to the book "The Good Society" by the American journalist Walter Lippmann, the concept of neoliberalism emerged when the question arose as to how a liberalism renewed for the 20th century should look. With the legacy of the classic liberalism of the 19th century, most of the participants were strongly critical. The two great ideas of the 19th century, nationalism and socialism, which at the time were being combined in a particularly sinister way in Germany, had won the battle of ideas, according to the interpretation of most of the participants, because the liberalism of the late 19th and early 20th century had become complacent and could find no answers to the central challenges facing the modern world.

In 1947, a meeting was held on the shores of Lake Geneva which, to some extent, could be regarded as a continuation of the internal liberal discourse that had begun in 1938.[2] The assembled thinkers, many of whom had been present in Paris, were now able to debate with renewed optimism about the positive programme of the liberalism renewed for the 20th century – and they continue to do so today in the Mont Pèlerin Society founded there. Apart from a small group that insisted on the laissez-faire of classical liberalism, there was consensus in the early years of the Society between Friedrich August von Hayek, German ordoliberals such as Walter Eucken and Wilhelm Röpke, as well as representatives of the Chicago School such as Frank Knight and the young Milton Friedman, that the core of renewed liberalism could be captured by the keywords "laissez-faire within rules". These neoliberals were interested in finding a framework within which the results of freedom in economy and society turned out to be productive in the material sense and, of at least equal importance, humane in an ideal sense.

Some of these neoliberals were still active in the 1970s and 1980s, when the Thatcher-Reagan revolution came into being in the US and Britain. The fact that these two politicians or, in a greatly modified form, Pinochet in Chile[3], were referring to Hayek and Friedman, led henceforth to the results of economic policy the US and UK being treated with hostility as "neoliberal" –

---

2   Cf. Caldwell, Bruce (Ed.): Mont Pèlerin 1947: Transcripts of the Sessions of the Founding Meeting of the Mont Pèlerin Society, Stanford: Hoover Institution Press 2022.

3   For detailed and differentiated analyses of Hayek and Friedman's visits to Chile, see Caldwell, Bruce/Montes, Leonidas: "Friedrich Hayek and His Visits to Chile", in: Review of Austrian Economics 28:3 (2015), pp. 261–309; Edwards, Sebastian/Montes, Leonidas: "Milton Friedman in Chile: Shock Therapy, Economic Freedom, and Exchange Rates", in: Journal of the History of Economic Thought 42:1 (2020), pp. 105–132.

even going as far the notion that we were living in a neoliberal world. The fact that, for example, the deregulation of the aviation industry began under Jimmy Carter, or that ideas are by no means the only driver of economic policy, was and is still not always important. To this day, it is still common practice in many languages for the reforms that people themselves dislike to be labelled as "neoliberal". Whether it's turbocapitalism, unleashed globalisation, entrenched digitisation or even social Darwinism: For many, it's all simply neoliberal.

The history of liberalism as a succession of forms of neoliberalism

The above juxtaposition clearly shows that the definition of the concept *in terms of content* is not quite so simple today. But a *procedural* look at it does provide a helpful impetus for today's liberalism. Historically, it is not correct to say that the term was coined in the 1930s. Rather, it is already found in the early 19th century in France[4] or in the late 19th century in Italy[5]. Already, these two data points indicate that there have been continued attempts to update liberalism for one's own time. In line with this interpretation, liberalism is a doctrine which may have a fixed core, but which takes on new forms in the different contexts of time and space. Strictly speaking, the history of liberalism could be seen as a succession of forms of neoliberalism, in the course of which new generations in their cultural spaces have constantly sought appropriate forms of contemporary liberalism. In this sense, Adam Smith is a neoliberal vis-à-vis John Locke, for example, and Wilhelm von Humboldt is a neoliberal vis-à-vis Smith and Locke.

As mentioned at the beginning, the author of the essay deliberately chooses "neoliberal" as his self-designation – and not "classical liberal", for example, as is customary for many members of the Mont Pèlerin Society, of which the author is also a member. This is due both to some shortcomings of "classical liberal" and to some advantages of "neoliberal". If something is declared to

---

4   Cf. "Neoliberalism turns eighty", in: Frankfurter Allgemeine Sonntagszeitung (FAZ on Sunday), August 12, 2018, p. 22.
5   Cf. Kolev, Stefan: "Paleo- and neoliberals: Ludwig von Mises and the 'ordo-interventionists'", in: Patricia Commun and Stefan Kolev (Ed.): Wilhelm Röpke (1899–1966): A Liberal Political Economist and Conservative Social Philosopher, Cham: Springer 2018, pp. 65–90.

be classical, this is done in an effort to put it on a pedestal and then to emulate it – as with classical music, for example. This poses dangers for liberalism which can nowadays be observed in very concrete terms. The emulation or even the adoration of the classical easily leads to dogmatism, the formation of sects or even of cults, as for example today with the many worshippers of Ayn Rand or Ludwig von Mises. Moreover, the term "classical liberal" is extremely vague: How much of Locke, how much of Smith and how much of Humboldt is in this amalgam exactly? "Neoliberal", on the other hand, involves a rhetoric that encourages today's liberals to deal with the history of liberalism *respectfully* whilst simultaneously thinking *innovatively* about a liberalism for the 21st century which is appropriate for today's socio-economic challenges. And this is indeed urgent, as a glance at the fragility of our present-day liberal order imperatively dictates.

Why we need a new neoliberalism today

The fact that history does not repeat itself, but quite probably rhymes, is a healthy attitude to the need for the renewal of today's liberalism. There is certainly much to learn from constellations of the past, such as the 1930s or 1980s. The 1930s bring to mind that "thinking in orders" is particularly helpful in moments of fragility of the order, both for understanding and for shaping the socio-economic reality. The 1980s help us to realise that there are still "empires of evil" today, and that the concepts of order in today's Russia or China are exactly that from a liberal point of view. Fortunately, many things are different today from how they were then. Globalisation has reached a level that is not comparable to the inter-war period or the early post-war decades, despite recent setbacks that could significantly change its character. In spite of current risks, digitisation has given all the citizens of the world access to knowledge, news or even specific services in a way that can historically be regarded as uniquely egalitarian. Yet the enthusiasm for this global digital world is anything but undivided, and the opponents of liberalism have become more diverse. Above all, the national and international orders of economy and society have become somewhat fragile, in a way that has no longer been perceptible since the inter-war period, at least in the West.

The new neoliberalism must be a liberalism capable of learning. It needs to manage to extract the "correct" – or, to use Walter Eucken's theoretical order terminology, "current" – knowledge from the various neoliberalisms of the past and, with particular historical caution, to transfer it to today's contexts. One answer to the old neoliberal question of the 1930s – as to which are the appropriate forms of a new neoliberalism – seems to be particularly relevant today: a liberalism that enables the individual to cope with the seemingly unbelievable dynamics of the emerging global digital order. The wonderful thing about the modern age is the dynamic exchange processes between billions of subjects in economy and society. But these exchange processes can also be overwhelming, especially when technology and economy are subject to such rapid change, as is the case today.

What makes the history of neoliberalism so fascinating is the constant search for institutions that make the dynamics of modernity humane. The state, with all its complexity, offers a variety of such institutions, and civil society does the same.[6] In today's order, they must above all serve as "benchmarks", i.e. as points of reference, which offer the individual a minimum level of stability and static equilibrium – or, to use the sociological power terminology of Heinrich Popitz, "security of order" – in the midst of the overwhelming global digital dynamic.[7] These can be educational opportunities, so that we can be certain to be able to make up quickly for the loss of human capital caused by globalisation or digitisation. Or instruments of environmental and climate protection which show that these phenomena are complex but nevertheless manageable. Or data protection measures which show how a minimum level of autonomy is possible in a digital coexistence. Or reforms of democratic practice which make use of digital technologies and show how one's own democratic participation in liberal civil society leads to an active contribution to the global digital order.

Liberals are often rightly fascinated by the open processes of open society. History teaches us that this openness has repeatedly been able to disrupt the fundamentally fragile order of the modern age. To prevent this from happening, open processes must be embedded in well-designed institutional forms that can be constantly re-balanced. The somewhat bulky and almost untranslatable term "Ordnungspolitik" (regulatory policy) of the German neoliberals of the Freiburg School does not stand in any way for a special German path,

---

6 Cf. Kolev, Stefan: A Comparison of Neoliberal State Concepts, Berlin: De Gruyter 2017.
7 Cf. Popitz, Heinrich: Phenomena of Power. Tübingen: Mohr Siebeck 1992/2009. See also the Centre for Liberal Modernity project "Security in Times of Rapid Change". https://libmod.de/en/report-security-in-times-of-change/

but instead for the central challenge of the history of liberalism (and its scientific sister, the history of political economy): to regulate freedom in a humane way. From a liberal point of view, we are living today in the best of all possible worlds. Let us hope that, with the help of a renewed liberalism, it will be possible for them to become a little less fragile in the future.

Do We Need a New Liberalism of Fear?

Amichai Magen

Liberalism – a term long subjected to much conceptual-stretching and abuse – is a political persuasion devoted to the pursuit of human flourishing through the exercise of individual liberty, economic openness, limited and egalitarian government, and the rule of law. At its core resides an insistence upon the sublime worth and dignity of each and every individual human being, and ultimately of life itself.

Liberalism's overriding political mission is to secure the essential conditions necessary for the fullest possible expression of that sublime individual worth, and the unique human potential imbued in it. It therefore rejects any political doctrine or system of government that does not respect the difference between the spheres of the personal and those of the state, between areas of individual private life (including family and communal life) and that of public authority.

At a minimum, liberalism demands, every individual must be permitted to write her own life's story – unobstructed by fear, cruelty, or crushing intrusion – as is compatible with the like freedom of every other individual. The life story written by the individual may amount to a heroic drama, a bitter-sweet comedy, or a tragic flop. Liberalism does not insist on a happy ending; but it does insist that it must, to a meaningful extent, be her story to write for herself.

Liberalism, in other words, is an essentially modern political quest for an existence in which human beings need not fear annihilation, arbitrary violence, unnecessary coercion, or violation of what Isaiah Berlin – in his Oxford Don's conspicuous understatement – described as "a certain minimum area of personal freedom which must on no account be violated."[1]

---

1 Isaiah Berlin, "Two Concepts of Liberty", in Four Essays on Liberty.Oxford: Oxford University Press1969. pp. 118–172 at pg. 122.

The liberalism of fear

This "Liberalism of Fear" – which Montesquieu and Constant already alluded to, but which was only explicitly illuminated and explored in Judith Shklar's brilliant 1989 chapter by the same name – is not the only species in the liberal tradition worth mining for ideas for twenty-first century liberal renewal.[2] Shklar recognizes this herself, referring to other types of liberalism, notably "the liberalism of natural rights" and "the liberalism of personal development", that differ from the liberalism of fear.[3]

One more caveat is noteworthy before I proceed to outline a case for a "New Liberalism of Fear", as one avenue for liberal renewal. "Fear" is, on its face, an unattractive prop for the liberal persuader. The smell of fear is normally understood to be odious. Hope, unicorns, and the promise of free love are, understandably, the preferred marketing tools of the political soothsayer.

The liberalism of fear, consequently, suffers from an inherent marketing problem. In this sense it is a little like Isaiah Berlin's notion of "Negative Freedom" – wise but not catchy.[4] The average consumer of political ideas will find no fluffy comfort in the liberalism of fear. What distinguishes it from those other types of liberalism, Shklar herself tells us, is that it is entirely "nonutopian".[5]

The liberalism of fear stares terror squarely in the face and shudders. It is starkly aware of the depths of depravity human beings are capable of and the scale of savagery and destruction that can be inflicted upon us fragile humans, particularly by institutionalized cruelty.

The liberalism of fear is defined by a certain terrible modesty of expectations. It is the liberalism of damage control, and of the good enough to get by. It is the liberalism of avoiding Auschwitz-Birkenau, the Soviet Gulag, and, in our own time, the brutalization of the Yazidis, the starvation of the Yemenites, or the prison camps of North Korea and Xinjiang. Its primary – and in some

---

2 On Montesquieu's reference to the human need for personal security as a precondition for political freedom see: Montesquieu, The Spirit of the Laws, tr. Cambridge: Cohler, Miller, and Stone1989, p. 157. Benjamin Constant also reflects on the relationship between security, fear, and liberty in his 1819 lecture The Liberty of the Ancients Compared with That of the Moderns. Judith N. Shklar, "The Liberalism of Fear", in Liberalism and the Moral Life, ed. Nancy L. Rosenblum.Harvard 1989, pp. 21–38.
3 Shklar, ibid., p. 26–27.
4 Berlin, Supra, note 1.
5 Ibid., p. 26.

respects primal – aim is to remind us to focus on avoiding the very worst that can happen to us, not assume that it somehow won't happen, or be tempted by the alluring but false utopian promises of a world free of tragedy.

A liberalism of damage control

The "New Liberalism of Fear" begins with the shaking-off of the historical amnesia that has pervaded our culture since 1989. Complacent, smug, and more than a little naïve, we slumbered under the warm duvet of post-1989 triumphalism. Confident that the end of history had arrived, that the arc of the moral universe was inexorably bending towards justice, and that the rest of the world would inevitably converge around an ever-expanding, ever-deepening Liberal International Order underwritten by the land of the free and the home of the brave.

Under the influence of this Fukuyama Coma, liberalism was permitted to stagnate and decay. Ironically, we liberals committed the cardinal sin of Marxism, the sin of historical determinism. We drifted, and largely squandered the hard won peace dividend that came from victory in the mighty ideological struggles against Fascism, Nazism, and Soviet Communism over the course of the bloody twentieth-century. We neglected to nurture the virtues, values, and institutions upon which modern liberal democracies depend for their survival – active and engaged citizenship, effective statehood and robust public institutions, genuine democratic accountability to ensure governments act in the interest of the majority, and the rule of law to constrain those who would wield coercive political, economic, and cultural power.

In the process, we left many of our fellow citizens behind – foolishly forgetting the first principle of liberal modernity, namely that the consent of the governed is the only solid basis for a functioning democratic order. We pretended that the dark sides of globalization were either not there, did not matter too much (that they would soon melt away under the forces of liberal convergence), or that they could be effectively managed by the invisible hand of markets alone. We neglected to keep up with accelerating connectivity, complexity, and disruptive, anxiety-inducing technological change. We failed to generate convincing liberal solutions to large emerging threats – Chinese authoritarianism, environmental damage, uncontrolled migration, failed states, nuclear proliferation, pandemics, unaligned Artificial Intelligence, and a degraded information ecology that risks obliterating our ability to agree on basic scientific and historical facts.

The "New Liberalism of Fear" demands a strongly developed sense of historical memory, and an historically-informed imagination about the future of humanity. It would therefore bring history back in, in three distinct ways:

First, to paraphrase Hal Brands and Charles Edel, it would insist that an understanding of tragedy remains indispensable to the conduct of politics, statecraft, and the preservation of world order.[6] If we forget the inherent fragility of liberal orders – and the need to continuously defend, preserve, and update them – we will invariably continue to sink into neglect and decline.

Making the case for the morality of liberal orders

Second, it would invest real time and energy in making the case for the morality (yes, morality, not just efficiency) of liberal orders. It would proudly champion and celebrate the astonishing human progress achieved since the birth of the liberal era, and especially over the past several decades, across all the main indicators of human material wellbeing, where liberal values and institutions took root. It would highlight the truly stunning 3,000 percent increase in real GDP for the poorest people since 1800, and how in the past three decades most of this "Great Enrichment" has occurred not in "white America" or Western Europe, but in liberalizing Latin America, Eastern Europe, China, India, and increasingly Africa.[7]

The "New Liberalism of Fear" would actively seek to make living and succeeding generations grasp the true meaning – in terms of human lives saved, improved, enriched, and liberated – of the following statistics: In 1950 global average life expectancy was less than 30 years, today it is 72.6. In 1950 global child mortality was 24 percent – meaning that nearly one in four babies died before their fifth birthday – today it is 4 percent. In 1950 the percentage of the

---

6   C.f. Hal Brands and Charles Edel, The Lessons of Tragedy: Statecraft and World Order, New Haven: Yale University Press 2019.

7   For the full data see The Maddison Project Database 2020 (available: https://www.rug.nl/ggdc/historicaldevelopment/maddison/releases/maddison-project-database-2020?lang=en). For a summary and analysis see: Deidre N. McCloskey, Bourgeois Equality: How Ideas, Not Capital or Institutions, Enriched the World, Chicago University Press 2016; Steven Pinker, Enlightenment Now: The Case for Reason, Science, Humanism, and Progress, New York: Viking 2018.

world's population living in extreme poverty was 63.5 percent, today it is less than 9. And in 1950 only 10 percent of the world's population lived in democracies, today – even after a decade and a half of a global democratic recession – 56 percent of human beings live in democracies.[8] This is an astonishing record of material and moral progress. It is imperfect, incomplete, and fragile, but it is also incalculably good and deserving of our gratitude, protection, and continued development.

Lastly here, the "New Liberalism of Fear" would make the case that rethinking liberalism must involve an expansion of our historical imaginations not just with reference to the past – with its litany of successes and failures, triumphs and crimes – but towards the future. Rethinking liberalism, as Toby Ord's wonderful dedication in his book The Precipice puts it, must involve a commitment: "To the hundred billion people before us, who fashioned our civilization; To the seven billion now alive, whose actions may determine our fate; To the trillions to come, whose existence lies in the balance."[9]

Living in fear makes us unfree

The question of whether or not we live in a free society, the "New Liberalism of Fear" understands, is to a great extent a matter of collective psychology. "We fear a society of fearful people" as Shklar puts it, because systematic mass fear makes human freedom impossible.[10] If we live in fear, we are fundamentally unfree.

High-tech tyranny of the type offered by the Chinese Communist Party might be more "efficient" than the politics of imperfection, individual choice, and uncertainty offered by liberalism. But what is the use of such efficiency to the human spirit? What is the point of it if it would make us into a gargantuan colony of fearful, cowering slaves? Similarly, what is the point of our human civilization if we make our planet uninhabitable or permit unaligned AI to run amok and hurl us into slavery or even extinction? The "New Liberalism of Fear"

---

8   Figures drawn from Our World in Data (available: https://ourworldindata.org/a-histo ry-of-global-living-conditions-in-5-charts). On life-expectancy see: https://ourworldi ndata.org/life-expectancy#:~:text=The%20divided%20world%20of%201950,achiev ed%20in%20a%20few%20places
9   Toby Ord, The Precipice. Existencial Risk and the Future of Humanity. Bloomsbury 2021.
10 Shklar, Supra, note 3, at p. 29.

stares into that soulless abyss of possible dystopian traps and shudders. It refuses to go gentle into those nightmarish nights. It rages against the dying of the light.

Liberals have feared different things at different times and so have striven to create and adapt political orders to tackle a succession of changing fears. Early modern liberalism – and there existed no liberalism in the pre-modern world – emerged from the chaos and carnage of religious intolerance and war. Fear of religious coercion is the cradle of modern liberalism. Gradually, over the course of the sixteenth and seventeen centuries, we discovered that toleration was superior to the cruelty of religious fanaticism.

Then, in a second grand wave of competition over the nature of political order, the principles and institutions of limited and egalitarian government proved to provide superior advantages – military, economic, scientific, and in terms of personal happiness – compared with Absolutism. Once Leviathan was firmly established, we discovered that it could devour us with greater ease and system than pre-modern authorities ever could. We therefore gradually then invented various mechanisms for taming Leviathan. We call these, variably, civil and political rights, the rule of law, constitutionalism, federalism and, eventually, modern representative democracy. Those societies who adopted and practiced these mechanisms sensibly achieved greater power, prosperity, and dynamism.

And from the turn of the twentieth century, our liberal orders – national, regional, and international – evolved again because we came to fear poverty, total war, and the rise of collectivist totalitarian ideologies and states. Spurred by these fears, nation-state based, market-based liberal democracies contested, and eventually defeated, their imperial, fascist, Nazi, and Soviet Communist adversaries.

Viewed through this prism, contemporary liberal orders are essentially a "triple-distilled" package of normative and institutional goods, accrued over centuries in a series of historical competitions where "the liberal solution" eventually emerged victorious, having proved superior to its competitors at providing physical and ontological wellbeing. Our modern forms of liberal order – containing the genome of toleration, bounded-statehood, consent-based representative democracy, and the market-economy – are the outcome of repeated successful contestation and selection. Liberal order has survived and proliferated because it has repeatedly proven superior in providing physical and ontological security. At the same time, the evolutionary logic is a cold one. Unless liberal orders are able to once again compete and demonstrate their superiority, we should expect anti-liberal order-contestation and defections to increase.[11]

The fear of human redundancy

What do we fear most today? In some places we still fear what Locke, Constant, Mill, Popper, Hayek, Arndt, Berlin, Solzhenitsyn and Shklar feared in the past – the unequal power of the authoritarian and predatory state over the individual. And yet, the "New Liberalism of Fear" would admit – with a pinch of skepticism mixed with cautious satisfaction – that in most contemporary societies, most of the time, it is not state power that we fear most. Indeed, in many areas of limited statehood – in Iraq and Libya, Syria, Somalia, Congo and Haiti, to name but a few sorry examples – it is the consequences of the absence of effective statehood that people fear most.

Ultimately, what we – in what until recently was lightly called "The Free World" – now fear most is a coming human redundancy. We fear physical redundancy as the result of existential catastrophes – demographic decline, climate extinction, unrecoverable civilizational collapse, or unrecoverable dystopia – at the hands of nature or anthropogenic threats. We fear the complete loss of economic and political human agency to uncontrolled forces of financial markets, Big-Tech algorithms, and ubiquitous corporate and state surveillance. We fear metaphysical redundancy in the loss of meaning, purpose, belonging and attachment, not so much to industrial-age alienation but to digital era machines and synthetic biology. We even fear epistemic redundancy, in that very soon AI and Deep Fake technologies may very well extinguish ordinary people's ability to handle the accelerating complexity of the world or tell the difference between fact and conspiracy theory.

The challenge before us liberals today is nothing less than to stem and reverse human redundancy. We require a new humanistic liberalism that is at once true to the core values of the liberal tradition and provides superior outcomes of human flourishing to those proffered by our authoritarian and collectivist adversaries.

The challenge posed by the "New Liberalism of Fear" is serious, possibly existential, but it is not entirely grim. As Bernard Williams observed in his

---

11   C.f. Amichai Magen, Liberal Order in the Twenty-First Century: Searching for Eunomia Once Again, 139/2–4 Journal of Contextual Economics (2019), pp. 271–284.

own meditation upon Judith Shklar's text: "the liberalism of fear is not confined to uttering warnings and reminders. If indeed primary freedoms are secured, and basic fears are assuaged, then the attentions of the liberalism of fear will move to more sophisticated conceptions of freedom..."[12] Confronting our era's worst fears squarely, resolutely, and creatively is arguably our best path forward to once again reach a liberalism of hope.

---

12   Bernard Williams, In the Beginning Was the Deed: Realism and Moralism in Political Argument, Princeton: Princeton University Press 2005, p. 60.

"Move Forward to the Back":
The Illiberal Turn in East-Central Europe

Jacques Rupnik

> »The liberal non-democracy is over.
> What a day! What a day! What a day!«[1]
> *Viktor Orban*

»Move forward to the back!«, this is an injunction that I heard once in a tramway in Warsaw. I propose to make it the rallying call of a powerful international that will never see the light of day.[2] That is the opening line of a memorable piece by Leszek Kolakowski entitled »How to be a conservative-liberal-socialist«.

Well, »Move forward to the back« could indeed be an appropriate heading to examine the recent regression of liberal democracy in Kolakowski's native Poland and other parts of East-Central Europe, over three decades after the end of communist rule and almost twenty years after joining the European Union.

»Rückschlag«, regression, is the term Oskar Jaszi, the Hungarian political thinker, used in the 1920's for his country under the Horthy regime, borrowing a term from psychoanalysis: in times of crisis old structures return to the fore. The old structures nowadays returning to the fore are not those of the Communist era, as some would have us believe, but perhaps, older, pre-communist ones, which resurface in the discourse and the political practice.

When Jaroslaw Kaczyński and Viktor Orbán, the leaders of Poland and Hungary, met in Krynica in the Fall of 2016, they celebrated Brexit and called

---

1 Viktor Orban, interview by Peter Foster, *The Daily Telegraph*, November 11, 2016. Interview given the day after the election of Donald Trump as US president.
2 Leszek Kolakowski, « Comment être conservateur libéral socialiste » *Commentaire* (n 4 – Winter 1978–79).

for a "counter-revolution" in Europe. In the old days, dissidents from Solidarnść and Charter 77 would meet on the Poslish-Czechoslovak border to devise democratic strategies for the opposition. Nowadays, two former dissidents, representing two countries long considered as the success-stories of post 1989 transformation of East-Central Europe, meet in the Tatra mountains to call for a "counter-revolution" in Europe.

The illiberal regression affects institutions and procedures of liberal democracy

The illiberal regression affects the countries of the region unevenly and is marked primarily by the erosion of key institutions and procedures of liberal democracies, most importantly the separation of powers and the rule of law (the independence of the judiciary). A related feature of the process is an assault on the independent media: public broadcasting is controlled by the government in both countries though some independent private media remain influential in Poland. Particularly in Hungary and Poland, to a lesser degree elsewhere, basic principles and values of liberal democracy are being challenged.

"The new state that we are building is an illiberal state, a non-liberal state. Just because something is not liberal it does not mean it is not democratic."[3] Viktor Orbán made a name for himself in 2014 speech by borrowing the concept of "illiberal democracy" from Fareed Zakaria to "theorize" his regime's drift toward authoritarianism.

What Zakaria meant as a warning against the proliferation of regimes with elections but without the rule of law, has been reclaimed as a virtue by a series of very assertive conservative critics of liberalism (among the Polish authors let us mentions Legutko, Krasnodebski, Cichocki, Wildstein). Liberal insistence on constitutionalism, checks and balances and the rule of law is presented as a means to obstruct the sovereignty of the people by elites associated with the EU or non-elected, allegedly politically neutral institutions such as the Constitutional court or the Central bank. In Kaczyński's words the aim is to break the straitjacket of "constitutional impossibilism". The flip side of unconstrained popular sovereignty is national sovereignty. Nation-states must remain the key

---

3   Viktor Orbán, "Speech at the XXV Bálványos Free Summer University and Youth Camp," Băile Tuşnad, July 26, 2014. http://budapestbeacon.com/

subjects of domestic and foreign policy. An ethnically defined nation protected from external intrusions be they migrants of EU institutions.

»The dog that did not bark«

How did we get from there to here, from 1989 as a transition to liberal democracy to the "illiberal temptation" of the last decade?

To be sure, there had been early warnings by leading Polish intellectuals. Bronisław Geremek, the historian and prominent figure of the Polish democratic opposition, warned in June 1990 of three dangers facing the new democracy in the making. First, populism associated with a widespread "egalitarian illusions". Second, "the temptation to instore strong-hand governments" and third: nationalism, a powerful force of collective resistance to communism which, in a destabilized society, could turn into chauvinism. Adam Michnik, a leading figure of Polish dissident movement and since 1990, editor of *Gazeta* daily, warned at a conference in Krakow in the Spring of 1991 against the threats of nationalist fundamentalism seeking to constrain the democratic debate, and of religious fundamentalism, that is the temptation to obliterate the division between a religion and a secular public sphere. Finally, there is the populist "them vs us" mindset inherited in a society after decades of opposition to a totalitarian state which is not the most conducive to pluralism.

These warnings did not materialize and we discarded them in the category of "the dog that did not bark". Hungary and Poland were considered the success stories of the post-1989 transition and together with the Czechs, then Slovaks, the Slovenes and the Balts joined the EU in 2004 then considered as the completion of their democratic transition. So how to account for the anti-liberal backlash? Several by no means mutually exclusive explanations can be suggested.

Five hypotheses for the illiberal backlash

First hypothesis: The most widespread in the Western discussion of the rise of populism has a socio-economic backbone and can be summed up as "winners vs losers" of the post-89 transitions which neatly complements the argument about the losers of globalization and the erosion of the middle-class support for liberalism. To be sure, there are undeniable important regional differences and the big divide between the capital and large cities in contrast to small town and rural areas which did not see the benefits or the trickle-down effect of the country's prosperity. The liberal free-marketeers in power (Balcerowicz in Poland, Klaus in the Czech Republic or Bokros in Hungary) in East-Central Europe for almost 20 years neglected the social question which was later captured by Fidesz and PiS when they came to power with generous handouts. The socialist parties' decline is also related to this paradox: they became culturally "Left" (liberal) and economically "Right" (pro-market); and the other way around for the conservatives who moved culturally further to the right and to the "Left" on socio-economic issues. So, the argument goes, the populist backlash against political liberalism is the price to pay for its collusion with economic liberalism.

Second hypothesis concerns liberalism challenged by nationalism. The 2015 migration crisis acted as a catalyst (not the cause) in a powerful reassertion of identity politics based on an organic concept of the nation[4]. The important thing to recall here is that for historical reasons the prevailing concept of the nation in East-Central Europe was close to the German *Kulturnation* rather than a French type "civic nation". For old nations which lost statehood and whose "very existence was not obvious" (Kundera), i.e. could not be taken for granted, language, culture, religion which were the key ingredients of nationhood in the 19th century which later sought political recognition and statehood. The great Hungarian political thinker Istvan Bibo in his *The Misery of Small States of Eastern Europe* (1944), argues that democracy is in danger, indeed there is a threat of fascism, "when the cause of liberty comes into conflict with the cause of the nation". In other words, for nations of East-Central Europe whose statehood, indeed their very existence, is fragile, the collective freedom of the nation will prevail over individual freedoms that are the basis of liberal democracy. The prime duty of state power is thus to protect the nation (including its cultural identity), an argument all the more powerful in a context combining a massive migration wave and demographic decline.

The demographic panic, the fear of the "grand replacement" could be exploited all the more easily by the political elites (Orbán, Kaczyński, but also Fico in Slovakia or Babis in the Czech Republic) given the makeup of the population

---

4   The PiS program states: "The Nation is a real community connected by ties of language and by an entire semiotic system, culture, historical fate and solidarity". The "semiotic system" is obviously closely identified with Roman Catholicism.

clearly contrasting with that of Western Europe. World War Two, the population losses and displacements created homogeneous nation-states in the region. The cold-war iron curtain only reinforced this: you could not get out, but nor could you not get in. East-Central Europeans did not experience the migrations from former colonies to Western Europe. They do not share the latter's post-colonial guilt which, in their view, accounts for the acceptance of non-European migrants and liberal promotion of multiculturalism. In Orban's words "Either we shall have a national government, Hungary will remain Hungarian and we shall have a European Europe. Or we shall have an internationalist government which will be essentially formed by George Soros. And the country will become a land of migrants"[5].

Third hypothesis: Culture wars. In a book entitled *The Demons of democracy, the totalitarian temptation in a free society*, Ryszard Legutko, a prominent Polish conservative thinker and European Parliament member for PiS argues that today liberalism became a major threat, a view shared by a range of conservative ideologues. Communists, he says, were obsessed by class, the liberals by gender, sexual orientation and race. The aim, however, remains the same: the dissolution of the family, of the nation and of the Church. The post-89 liberal consensus is over, as Legutko argues, the EU now promotes a Left-liberal agenda including gay marriage, LGBT rights, abortion and multiculturalism, all of which have to be resisted. This discourse about the decadent Europe has some traction in the population which in the whole tends to be more conservative than in Western Europe. Societal liberalism represents a major divide within the countries of the region but also between them and those of Western Europe.

4th hypothesis: the historical and sociological weakness of liberalism in Eastern-Central Europe. Historically, liberalism has been an import from the West. There were socio-economic reasons such as the lesser development of cities, of a bourgeoisie often identified with German and Jewish minorities and the relative weakness of civil society.

There was a liberal-democratic political tradition going back to the post-1848 period. During the *Ausgleich* period (1867–1918) Hungarian gentry espoused liberalism with figures like the baron Josef Eötvös, the "Hungarian Tocqueville", and built a Parliament which was a copy of Westminster (only bigger!). But the Austro-Hungarian liberal tradition did not survive the empire: the Hungarian liberals were silenced by the trauma of Trianon (the loss 1/3 of the Hungarians living in successor states); the Austrians moved to America

---

5   Radio Kossuth, April 6, 2016.

(Hayek, von Mises, Schumpeter) where they became key figures of the Chicago school of free-marketeers. The Czechs had their liberal moment during the 1st republic (1918–38) under the philosopher-king Tomas Masaryk, but it did not survive Munich and its betrayal by Western liberal democracies, Britain and France. Most other ECE lands in the interwar period gradually moved towards semi-authoritarian regimes.

Politically and philosophically, liberalism was revived only in the 1970's with the demise of Marxism after the defeat of the Prague Spring and the emergence of dissident and the human rights movements. They rehabilitated the language of rights (as opposed to revisionist squabbles about the (im)possibility of improving socialism) and rehabilitated the importance of civil society in the struggle against dictatorship. 1989 was thus clearly framed as a liberal democratic revolution with its triple dimension: rights and the rule of law, civil society as an indispensable component of democratic renewal, and Europe as a goal and indispensable anchor for the new democracies.

However, the ex-dissident intellectuals were soon eclipsed, and their liberal legacy discarded. Václav Havel as Czech president stood for liberal values even as the real power was in the hands his main rival and later successor, Václav Klaus, a disciple of Margaret Thatcher (markets, strong nation-state and "there is no such thing as society") who later turned into a supporter and guest-speaker at a congress of AfD. Viktor Orban started as a 1989 liberal sent for a semester with a Soros scholarship to study the concept of civil society at Oxford. Now civil society is curtailed in Hungary and Karl Popper's notion of an *Open society* became a dangerous tenet of liberal ideology: "Open society is perhaps the most influential and most destructive conclusion of post-World War II Western thinking. Its importance is extraordinary, as today open society – we can safely say – is the West's only intellectual school of thought that can be regarded as ideologically consistent. " (Corvinus university speech 2018). People want "democratic not open societies", concludes Orban.

5th hypothesis: The end of the post-1989 liberal cycle. If the 1989 agenda was democracy, market economy and Europe, one could, on the 20th anniversary, declare "mission accomplished". With one proviso: all three tenets were in crisis. The following decade only completed what seemed clear by then: the liberal post-1989 cycle was exhausted.

It would be misleading, however, to see this as a mere "Eastern" aberration which feeds belated doubts about the wisdom of EU's Eastern enlargement to countries some of which today openly challenge its founding principles such as the rule of law. Indeed, the rise of populist challenge to liberalism has in recent years come from some of the countries such as the US or the UK considered as key post-war anchors of liberal democracy. With Trump and Brexit, Orban, Kaczynski and a few others felt vindicated. They were no longer the East European laggards, but rather the 'vanguard' of populist nationalism which has shaken the post-1989 liberal order.

The limits of illiberalism

There are, however, important limitations to the illiberal drift. If the aim of Orbán and Kaczyński is to reshape the European political landscape with the likes of Salvini and Le Pen, then the transeuropean nature of the problem highlights crucial role played by the resilience of EU institutions and the political will to stand by the values and principles on which it has been founded.[6]

Belatedly, this may now be happening. For the first time in its history, the EU has invoked article 7 of the Lisbon treaty that in theory could lead to suspend the voting rights of a member-state for major breaches of the rule of law. Given that this require unanimity, more effective may prove to be the recent decision to use conditionality for the access to EU funds for the post-covid recovery or from the so-called "structural funds" that are part of the overall EU budget and provide about 3% of the GDP of the countries concerned.

The second limit of the illiberal trend is to be found inside the societies of East-Central Europe. These countries are deeply divided and their politics highly polarized. True, Orban today has disciples and allies among the strongmen of Slovenia (Jansa) or Serbia (Vučić). But there is also mounting opposition. The Mayors of the cities of Budapest, Warsaw, Prague and Bratislava issued a joint statement in 2018 stating their opposition to the illiberal and Eurosceptic politics of their governments. The only way to defeat them is to form broad coalitions going from Left of center Greens to Right of center Christians around the defense of liberal principles. In Poland, such a coalition lost the presidential election in 2021 by 1%. In the Czech Republic a broad coalition has

---

6 Politics rather than the reliance on the decisions of the European Court of Justice. The latter has an important role to play in upholding the rule of law in member states, but its temptation to intervene on societal issues is contested even when invoking "European values" since they precisely are and will remain an object of controversy in the public sphere.

in 2021 defeated the populist entrepreneur Andrej Babiš in the general election. However, the crucial test for the region was the Hungarian election in April: Victor Orbán won again.

Finally, there is the geopolitical perspective. For the countries of East Central Europe, Brexit (or Polexit) is not really an option: when you see the destabilization and even war in your eastern neighborhood and the threats posed by an assertive Russia, you think twice before slamming the door of the EU even with its constraints. Do you prefer your sovereignty threatened by a powerful neighbor our do you prefer to share it within the EU?

In their rejection of EU concerns over the state of the rule of law in their countries, on a number of occasions, Orban and Kaczynski, and most explicitly the Polish and Hungarian ministers of justice, Zbigniew Ziobro and Judit Varga, have compared the European Union to the Soviet Union and Brussels to Moscow. This, of course, is outrageous and an insult to other Europeans who have for some 70 years developed the European project associated for them with peace, democracy and prosperity. The Visegrád countries have joined it freely after referenda and they know, as Brexit has shown, that you can also leave it.

The most powerful answer to the preposterous "Bussels is the new Moscow" claims came from Kiev, when president Selensky in a live address to the European Parliament said in substance: "We desperately want to join Europe because we want to become a liberal democracy of which the EU and the European Parliament are the embodiment". Between Russian autocracy and European liberal democracy, Orban and Kaczynski seemed in two minds. President Zielenski knows better. There is nothing like having Russian tanks invading your country to concentrate the minds.

Liberalism beyond Individualism and Capitalism

Christoph Möllers

In its two hundred year-old history, political liberalism has often changed, entering into very different political and economic coalitions. Originally the project of a political centre that wanted to preserve the achievements of the French revolutions from feudal restoration without becoming too revolutionary in turn, the liberals of the 19th century were the agents of an emerging middle class. Thus, they stood for modernisation and emancipation, without wanting to become too involved in the democratic reforms which were implemented against their resistance in the course of the 19th century through the introduction of universal suffrage. The electorate which was thereby increased ended the great period of political liberalism quite soon; liberal parties disappeared or were marginalised. Political liberalism became an establishment of political ideas that had to be divided between moderate parties from the right and the left, between which the liberal family was also split time and again. The fact that liberalism and democracy necessarily belong to one another was, based on the experiences in the 19th century, not a foregone conclusion. The fact that we now readily identify liberalism and democracy collectively in the West is a result of the post-war period and the Cold War. More and more, this equalisation is being denied by authoritarian rulers who invoke a supposedly democratic mandate for their illiberal practices.

Liberalism in changing coalitions

The economic preferences of liberal politics have also changed several times over the last two hundred years. The early and pre-liberals did not despise state regulation by any means, but as early as the first third of the 19th century, a form of liberalism critical of regulation came to the fore with "Manchester" liberalism, still infamous to this day, to be connected to social Darwinian models.

It is less well known that this idea was soon criticised by a regulatory-friendly "New Liberalism" and replaced by other models of state intervention in the economic cycle. Social liberal progressive thinking was all the rage in the UK around 1900. Moderately socialist and liberal political programmes cannot always be easily distinguished from one another before the First World War. The ideologically political capital here deserved to be raised and modernised again.

It is in turn not self-evident that liberalism and capitalism seem to be in such a firm alliance with each other at the present time: One reason for this today lies in a one-sided perception of liberal traditions of thought, which are often shortened to a special form of neoliberalism.[1] This is also the result of a conceptual political coalition: state-critical deregulators and privatisers have monopolised the term "liberal"; this suits left- and right-wing critics of liberalism, because they get a handy opponent to attack.

But the experience of the Cold War was also more important here than such conceptual volte-faces. With the Soviet-led Eastern bloc, the liberal-democratic West had an adversary which combined a lack of democratic legitimacy with a lack of efficient economic structures. In the Eastern bloc, the population was not only not free from the West's point of view, but also poor. This led to the conclusion that a necessary condition must exist between freedom and prosperity, and thus also between liberalism and capitalism.

The fact that such concordances are politically possible, but not necessary, only became apparent with the economic rise of the People's Republic of China, which liberal economists did not anticipate. With it, an economically efficient capitalist structure was established, whose political democratisation and liberalisation is today even more distant than at the beginning of the development in the 1980s. If no direct lessons for a future political liberalism can be learnt from the rise, then unfamiliar negative insights will be evident here for a long time. All of a sudden, it seems possible that the increase in general welfare may be at odds with individual or political freedoms. Even the connection between freedom and capitalism is no longer taken for granted in the 21st century. Illiberal capitalism exists. But the question is whether there can be free societies that function without at least a competitive economic order. There are no examples of this, as far as can be seen.

---

1   Cf. Kolev, Stefan: "Poison cupboard or treasure chest? Why each generation needs its own neoliberalism", in this volume.

The free individual and the free political community

The emphasis on *individual* freedom always seemed to have been a reasonably clear sign of liberal political practice. If you take a closer look, you will of course get a more complex picture. It is true that in liberal theory and practice, political rule should be regularly tied to the consent of individuals and serve their freedom. It is also true, however, that the political concerns associated with it were not originally directed against the authority of the state, but against feudal and intermediary structures, against guilds, associations and corporations. The liberal state authority created by individual consent would then perhaps be more rationally tamed than the monarchy, but certainly no less politically powerful. Liberalism – and this has often been misunderstood – created a political world in which the individual and political rule sought to strengthen each other.

The individual thus empowered was also, but not only, an economic entity. Concepts of a strong individual personality which forms and develops itself in many ways belong to a liberal self-image from the beginning – and accompany us up to the present day. In particular, the triumphal procession of fundamental and human rights as the least controversial normative building block of liberal systems today continues this normative individualism. Nevertheless, there is some reason to believe that our ideas of individual freedom are already in the midst of a conceptual upheaval that is also likely to have political significance. The reasons for this upheaval are likely to lie less in the authoritarian threat than in the insights that liberal societies have gained into themselves. Three examples of these should be mentioned:

The first insight lies in the close connection between inequality and a lack of freedom. The fact that social inequality does not only harm those who are actually affected, but also a community as a whole, is an insight that is still in its infancy. For example, unequal societies have greater problems with public health or corruption than egalitarian societies. The contrast between liberalism and egalitarianism, handed down by liberal theories, weakens in light of such insights. Even the observation that economic freedom and political involvement cannot be so clearly isolated from each other as liberal theories often suggest points in this direction. Uneven wealth creates unfree politics. The fact that freedom of expression protects someone who has a voice and someone who has a newspaper in the same way has always been a peculiar notion. The contrast between liberalism and egalitarianism which is upheld by traditional liberalism cannot be sustained in this way.

The second insight lies in the realisation that the development of individuality can always be understood only as a social achievement. To be free requires a lot, and everything that it requires must be learnt and preserved. But no individual is in a position to do this alone. For this reason, the idea that freedom consists in the absence of social and political design is not convincing for individual freedom either. This insight also has implications for the liberal – and as such not outdated – notion of fair competition. If liberalism cannot dispense with criteria of merit, it must correct its unequal conditions of production. The starting point for equal opportunities will therefore have to shift to the early childhood conditions of skills development. In this sense, the liberal idea of free competition has a high levelling potential, which contemporary liberalism must confront.

Thirdly and finally, the development of "ecological" thinking also challenges individual liberalism. If "ecology" develops models for the relations between living beings and their inanimate environment, this can also gain significance for political notions of individual freedom. Thus, tackling the climate crisis also requires a political epistemology that radically overcomes the notion of the atomised individual as a central entity.

Political implications of changed conditions of freedom

This means that we are now in a world in which it is not self-evident what a political liberal project might look like. It will simply not be able to invoke individual freedom and capitalist economies. On the other hand, it cannot do without a marked reference to individuality, which must nevertheless take up the challenges mentioned. The political implications associated with it are manifold.

In foreign policy, political liberalism must prepare itself for the fact that the enemies of liberalism are neither manageably definable, as was the case in the Cold War era, nor will they simply disappear, as could be believed in the post-1989 period of optimism. Political liberalism today is a politically threatened bloc in need of defence. Despite all the horrors that the Russian invasion of Ukraine has aroused, it has also created the necessary clarity about this connection. The typically liberal notion that one's own ideas would prevail because they were right is also political self-disempowerment. It will not be so easy to distinguish between friends and opponents – and the survival of liberalism will also depend on being politically stringent here and not leaving liberal regimes alone that stand in the shadow of illiberal systems – such as Ukraine or

Taiwan – not just out of solidarity, but for the sake of the survival of the entire project.

At home, these changes have far-reaching political consequences. These include the development of a liberal model of the criticism of capitalism, the development of models of an intelligent meritocracy that prevents the petrification of the elite, and the political formulation of the question of how to operationalise politically the difficult concept of "future generations". Liberalism will have to be reinvented once again, but it will also have to fall back on available instruments. One example would be the development of a structure of inheritance taxation which, while respecting certain limits of what is acquired within the family, addresses the enormous problem of perpetuating inequality through the acquisition of wealth that is not achieved through personal achievement. This presupposes, however, the realisation that the inequality created by inheritance also produces a substantial part of political inequality.

If this has caused political liberalism to enter a great state of flux, the question of the criteria which still hold them together in this matter is, of course, also open. The question of ideological consistency is often a more academic one, because political camps develop continuously without their identity always having to be challenged. Nevertheless, a concluding thought on this question should be formulated: If liberalism were to reinvent itself time and again based on the concept of freedom, then "political liberalism" – that is, one that is orientated towards possible political actions – should today be less orientated towards ideal models of a justified regime, as we have been shown in the theories of John Rawls and Jürgen Habermas, for example, than towards politically more concrete experiences of a lack of freedom. Political liberalism comes to the fore where people are denied the right to formulate and realise life plans, because this prevents political domination, social or economic powers or ecological living conditions.

Freedom and Justice in a Double Pack: A Short Journey through the Liberal Intellectual History of Justice

Karen Horn

One of the destructive patterns in political debates is thinking in rigid opposites. Thus, in some arguments during the coronavirus pandemic, individual freedom suddenly finds itself as an irreconcilable antithesis of solidarity, and occasionally one had the impression that an either-or relationship was being construed between health and prosperity. Even before that, it was not entirely unusual to set desirable values against each other, instead of asking what connects the two and how it could be realised in a double pack – for example self-interest and the common good, economy and ecology. Another example is freedom and justice. In the search for the connection, tensions may already be appearing. That is precisely where the path forks: Do I bring matters to a head or do I try to resolve them? Which direction you choose certainly has something to do with your personal temperament. But it is only thinking together which is constructive, not the radical, notoriously irreconcilable conceptual delimitation.

Hayek and social justice

The fact that the view of the two high values of freedom and justice in general is clouded by the idea of incompatibility has much to do with the neglect of the justice issue by some liberal thinkers and also with long-standing frontal attacks against essential aspects of justice. An unfortunate role is played here, for example, by the famous economist and social philosopher Friedrich August von Hayek, who sees justice essentially as an individual virtue and castigates any idea of a social dimension of justice beyond the pure rule of law as a category error. Thus, the second volume of his late work, "Law, Legislation and Freedom", bears the attention-grabbing subtitle "The Illusion of Social Justice".[1] For Hayek, the term social justice, as he puts it pointedly, belongs to the category of nonsense, similar to the expression "a moral stone". Many a Hayekian firebrand therefore still does not use the term, either on principle or at best writes it between mocking and ridiculous quotation marks – just as conservative West Germans once did with the abbreviation "GDR".

If Hayek's statements on "social justice" were to be taken at face value as a category error, it would mean that he was distancing himself drastically from the conceptual practices that have been common in philosophy since ancient times. In Plato's "Politeia", for example, justice occupies the rank of the "basis of all virtues".[2] It is discussed both in its individual and in its social forms, with the emphasis that, in the end, it is more recognisable "on a large scale", in other words in the context of society as a whole. However, influenced by Karl Popper's critical interpretation of totalitarianism, Hayek doesn't really have Plato much in mind. But Aristotle has both dimensions, too. They are both touched by the fundamental justice dilemma which Aristotle specifically expresses and which has challenged ethics ever since: What is just anyway – to each his own, whatever that may be, or to each the same? Does justice mean transactional justice – or rather distributive justice? You can guess the answer: It depends on the context, and the aspects overlap. So if you dismiss "social justice" from the outset as a mere category error, you have missed something. Above all, however, it is no wonder that the tables are turned in the discussion and, as is currently happening, individual freedom as a conceptual foreshortening falls into disrepute.

Hayek, however, goes further and more vehemently than is necessary for his argument and thus, regrettably, is promoting the ideological flattening and vulgarisation of his theory. Meanwhile, anyone who follows the commandment of accurate reading as well as intellectual mercy can quickly see that Hayek did not categorically deny a social dimension of justice. However, he sought to free it from the exclusive focus on the material results of the market process and to attract greater attention to its rules, in other words from distributive justice towards procedural justice. According to his theory, only general rules can be just – that is, rules that are as universal as possible, which exclude discrimina-

---

1   Hayek, Friedrich A. from: "Law, Legislation and Freedom", Tübingen: Mohr Siebeck 2003.
2   Plato: The State. Leipzig: Reclam 1985.

tion and thus correspond to the highest liberal principle, which is at the same time an egalitarian one: equal human dignity for all persons.

Procedures vs. market results

Market-based rules of procedure are well suited for this, because they guarantee general market access without regard to the person and also embed all participants equally in the purely economic logic and in this respect arbitrary, open-ended, "spontaneous order" of voluntary cooperation in competition. Competition is a powerful mechanism of social coordination and a prerequisite for the emergence of new knowledge in society. The problem with the focus on distributive justice, on the other hand, is that its ultimately arbitrary norms must logically anticipate, intervene in and distort the outcomes of this process, which is thought to be open – and thus weaken it in its capacity to coordinate people's economic plans and to allow the new knowledge necessary for progress to develop. This is Hayek's important, ongoing warning. The tendency should be towards being all the more convincing and compatible, since Hayek was in no way a supporter of a minimal state and by no means so radical as to deny the legitimacy of any democratically decided redistribution measure.

But the history of liberal ideas offers even more radical – and thus, at the same time, more closely guided – elements than the Hayekian theory of justice. These include some libertarian approaches that result in notions of a minimal state or anarcho-capitalism. They attribute justice solely to the fundamental moral rights of individuals. These, in turn, are derived to a greater or lesser extent from natural justice. They are focused on the protection of individual property, a logical consequence of man's self-ownership postulated by John Locke in his "Second Treatise on Government".[3] The right to the fruits of one's own labour is linked to this, as is the demand for free disposal of it, that is to say for freedom of contract. From this perspective, therefore, any action which the individual person curtails when determining his or own life or property is unfair. To this end, Murray Rothbard formulated the "non-aggression axiom" as a standard of justice.[4] Conceivable recipients of this standard are both one's fel-

---

3   Locke, John: Second Treatise on Government. Leipzig: Reclam 2012.
4   Rothbard, Murray: The Ethics of Liberty, Atlantic Highlands, NJ: Humanities Press 1982.

low human beings and the state. Therefore, there is also an individual ethical dimension here and a collective, institutionally ethical dimension of standards.

The non-aggression axiom

The non-aggression axiom may seem self-evident, but it is extremely restrictive, especially with regard to collective sovereign actions. For example, when interpreted purely and strictly, levying any taxes constitutes aggression and is therefore unjust, in the same way as with historical monument protection regulations for properties or the obligation to wear masks imposed by health policy during the pandemic: In all these cases, individuals finally experience a collective compulsion which limits or "attacks" their free disposal of themselves, their body or even their property. Another aspect that may not be so easily connected is the limitation of justice being merely a negative norm, that is to say, it requires an omission (of behaviour that is harmful to others), but not a positive action (active aid by an individual or also by the community, for example the welfare state). The non-aggression axiom formulates, as it were, only an individual ethical minimum standard. This does not exclude any further-reaching, proactive moral behaviour of the individual, but most libertarians do not see it as a duty, and certainly do not classify it under the rubric of justice. Ultimately, this is a problem of the allocation of terms. The degree of radicalism of libertarians depends on whether they can imagine circumstances in which the postulated rights of the individual can be overlapped or trumped by other moral aspects – as stated, for example, by Robert Nozick.[5] An example of this would be a general vaccination requirement, which radical libertarians must categorically dismiss as an assault on the person, while moderate liberals can justify it without much effort.

The fact that nomenclature often plays a confusing role is also illustrated by looking into Adam Smith's incomparably rich works.[6] As for his contemporary Immanuel Kant, he considers justice essential for the continued existence of society. But instead of following the path of obligatory ethics of justice derived from reason, Smith sees them, as did libertarians later on, as an essentially negative virtue which is primarily about not harming other people. The traces of Greek philosophy typical of Smith's work can also be identified. However,

---

5   C.f. Nozick, Robert: Anarchy, State, Utopia: Olzog 2011.
6   Smith, Adam: Prosperity of Nations. Cologne: Anaconda 2013.

he does not follow in the footsteps of Plato and Aristotle, but rather of Epicurus, according to whom justice is not to be derived in an abstract manner, but is ultimately based on an agreement by people not to harm one another. This agreement then gives rise to the right. According to Smith, this defensive imperative of justice is often satisfied by sitting still and doing nothing at all.

Therefore, justice demands an omission – both from the individual, who should do no wrong to others, and from the government, which must not deprive its citizens of their "natural freedom". For positive moral duties, Smith opens up another conceptual department, which he calls "beneficence".[7] Justice bears the social edifice, while beneficence is an additional ornament that beautifies the whole. For Adam Smith, as for Hayek later, beneficence is an important individual virtue, but not a normative category which can be increased on a collective scale in a meaningful way and which would be suitable for the orientation of state action. The state is not responsible for morality, but for the law which formalises the social convention of justice – which is always context-dependent – and which makes it legally enforceable and implementable. In other words: The logical place for justice within the state is the law. However, the law, whether found or laid down, is inevitably rooted in the changing moral understanding of people.

A forerunner of the warning against an "pretence of knowledge" that Hayek later put forward can already be found here from Smith: In the concrete case, informed by its perspective, man learns in his model from the interaction with others and the examination of his conscience, the "impartial observer", whether an active benevolent action is required beyond the passive, individual justice that avoids possible harm to other people. Smith outlines concentric circles of our ability, nurtured by our powers of imagination and familiarity, to put ourselves in the shoes of other people; just as concentric are the circles of our ability to do something good for them. The further away the specific case is from me, the less I know about the prevailing circumstances and the specific needs and wishes of the person concerned, the more emphatically my impartial observer, imagined in an exemplary way, advises me to stop – not that I would do the wrong thing with the best intentions! The government, on the other hand, cannot base its judgement of what would be of help to someone, and in what way it should behave benevolently, on its individual powers of imagination and close familiarity with the beneficiary, who is usually only a statistical number to them. Their judgement remains necessarily abstract.

---

7   Smith, Adam: Theory of Ethical Feelings. Hamburg: Meiner 2013.

It threatens to lump different people together and thereby allow injustice to befall all too many; therefore, it is bound to show restraint.

Rawls' Theory of Justice

From the thought, already touched upon by Epicurus and detailed in Adam Smith's model of empathetic feedback, that our ideas of justice are ultimately based on an agreement, it is no longer far from the liberal theory of justice that has been most explicit and carefully elaborated to date – John Rawls' contractualist theory of justice.[8] What justice is in its substance, Rawls derives from an individual rational benefit calculus which free, autonomous and equal citizens use for themselves. Rawls mentally puts people behind a "veil of ignorance" where they are unaware of their rank in society, their material endowment, their talents and inclinations – so that they can reach an impartial understanding of general rules rather than seeking only their pre-defined own advantage. Behind such a veil, Rawls expects people to agree on two principles of justice. Firstly: "Every person has an equal right to the most comprehensive system of equal fundamental freedoms, compatible with the same system of freedoms for all". And secondly: "Social and economic inequalities are acceptable if they are associated with (a) the greatest benefit to be expected for the most disadvantaged and b) positions and offices open to all under conditions of fair equality of opportunity."

Rawls' theory is an exciting, fruitful conception that incorporates many other elements from the multifaceted liberal history of ideas. It has the advantage of associating freedom and justice in a constructive way, rather than dividing them apart and thus manoeuvring itself into speechlessness. It is also valuable that it teaches us to look at the adequacy of the general rules, the rules of the game which affect us all and which were stressed by Hayek, but also by James M. Buchanan.[9] It points out that one's own interest is inextricably linked with the common good. But, of course, the devil is in the detail with this conception as well. It raises questions: How convincing is the thought experiment of the "veil"; can the control level and action level actually be separated? How

---

8 Rawls, John: A Theory of Justice, Revised Edition, *Cambridge*: Harvard University Press 1999.
9 Buchanan, James M.: The Collected Works of J. M. Buchanan. 20 Volumes, Indianapolis: Liberty Fund, Inc. 1999 – 2002.

realistic is it that economic freedom would also be part of the consensus? And must the fictitious unification behind the veil of ignorance not be followed by a public debate and an actual vote? Liberal philosophy has been working on this for decades. It is not a subject for the impatient.

Ecology and Freedom

Ralf Fücks

Climate policy has rather been a blind spot, or at least a weak point of the liberal school. Many liberals feel uncomfortable with the issue. They sense state paternalism and see the climate movement as a Trojan horse for taking markets under state control, restricting freedom of consumption and prescribing lifestyles.

Liberal parties tend to remain in the defence mode about climate policy, and among the younger generation they are suspected of playing down the problem of climate change and slowing down the necessary change. In Germany, the Liberal Party is the favourite opponent of the climate movement – Fridays for Future rallies are regularly held in front of the FDP party centre.

The retreat to the expansion of an emissions trading system and the CO_2 price as the central instrument of climate policy is apparently not enough to give liberals sufficient credibility, especially since many liberal parties shy away when it comes to actually raising the prices of fossil fuels sensitively – especially now that energy prices in Europe are exploding anyway.

If the advocates of a free economic order and an open society do not want to be increasingly on the defensive, they need more climate competence and convincing concepts of their own.

We should be under no illusions: Climate change is a litmus test for liberal democracy: Will we manage the rapid transition to climate neutrality and at the same time preserve the achievements of liberal modernity – or will we slide into a new era of commandments and prohibitions and a new kind of an "ecological planned economy" that distributes scarcity as fairly as possible? Or will we move forward towards ecological modernity, the unleashing of a new scientific and technological revolution and a new synthesis of man and nature? Those who set ecology and freedom against each other will lose both in the end.

Climate change heralds the end of an era. Like a sorcerer's apprentice, industrial modernity has set a process of global warming in motion. Since the unleashing of fossil energies, the average global temperature has risen by 1.1 degrees; we are currently moving towards 2.7 degrees by the end of this century. This would mean a dramatically changed world with precarious living conditions for billions of people.

At least in Europe, and increasingly in the USA, the debate on climate change and climate policy has reached a new stage. Phasing out coal, a fundamental change towards e-mobility and sustainable agriculture, greening our cities and reducing meat consumption is no longer a question of whether, but of how. This is now also true for large parts of the business world.

But there is much more at stake than the way we generate energy, produce food and run factories. With climate change, the expansive lifestyle of modernity is also coming under criticism. The more clearly the threat to the ecological foundations of life comes to light, the louder the call: "You must change your way of life!" For the advocates of a new, frugal lifestyle, climate change is the consequence of the expansive lifestyle of two billion people (the global middle class) who enjoy all the benefits of modernity without regard for the consequences. The pleasure of unlimited mobility, the large flat, the power-hungry online communication and the high meat consumption are all considered as ecological sins. In this view, our strive for "more and more" ruins the planet. "Repent and turn around!" is therefore the new categoric imperative.

The extroverted self-realisation of modernity was based on the seemingly unlimited availability of fossil fuels. They were the fuel for an enormous increase in production and consumption. Now that it has become clear that the burning of coal, oil and gas is upsetting the earth's climate, the hedonism of modernity is also coming under criticism. Its melody sounds convincing: a kind of freedom that is lived out at the expense of the rest of humanity becomes mere egoism. It destroys the freedom of future generations to live in a semi-intact environment. Instead of constantly expanding the limits of what is possible, we are now supposed to submit to the planetary boundaries. The age of "higher, faster, further" is over. The new ethic of limitation calls for decongestion and sufficiency. It is about to be instead of to have.

If one follows the logic of degrowth, then collective commandments and prohibitions must help when the appeal for moderation falls on deaf ears. They restrict the freedom of the individual in order to protect the lives of all. The imperative of restriction seems morally unassailable. Nevertheless, it is the wrong answer to climate change and species extinction. Ecologically, it is too short-sighted. Socially, it leads to growing polarisation. Politically, it leads to the slippery slope of an authoritarianism in the name of saving the world.

Ecological calvinism vs. the green industrial revolution

The German philosopher Peter Sloterdijk precisely predicted the new cultural struggle years ago:

> "The ethics of the future, which is hostile to expressions and emissions, aims straight at the reversal of the hitherto existing civilisation. (...) It demands minimization where previously maximization applied, it enjoins frugality where previously dissipation was seen as the greatest attraction, it calls for self-restraint where previously self-liberation was celebrated. If one thinks these reverse dynamics through to the end, one arrives at a kind of ecological Calvinism in the course of the meteorological reform."[1]

The struggle between the supporters of a morally based policy of restriction and those who see this policy as an attack on their way of life has a strong social bias, especially because the privileged children of the affluent society are calling for "a turn to the less". Therein lies the danger of a populist mobilisation of the "common people" against the wealthy advocates of an ecological policy of renunciation. It is no coincidence that the French "Yellow Vests Protests" was ignited by rising petrol prices.

The supporters of a restrictive environmental policy like to invoke the axiom "you can't negotiate with the climate". They refer to ecological constraints that are above politics. The roadmap to climate neutrality then results from seemingly exact tables of how much CO_2 the German electricity sector, industry, agriculture or the transport sector must cut back per year in order to keep global warming below two degrees Celsius. Apparently exact, because any isolated view of specific economic sectors is just as fictitious as a nationally limited strategy.

Such a "planned economy" climate policy misses the crucial point: the innovation dynamic that arises from the combination of modern science, the market economy and an active civil society. Politics must set targets, invest in the ecological renewal of infrastructure (energy grids, transport, urban development) and ensure that "prices tell the ecological truth" by introducing environmental taxes and expanding the European Emissions Trading Scheme.

---

1 Sloterdijk, Peter: What Happened in the 20th Century?: Towards a Critique of Extremist Reason. Cambridge: Polity 2018.

However, governments should be careful not to lay down the paths to climate neutrality in detail and to impose ever new commandments and prohibitions.

Those who seek the answer to climate change in the voluntary or forced restriction of production and consumption are not only falling short – they are heading in the wrong direction. In a shrinking economy, investments and the pace of innovation also decline. In the race against climate change, however, we need a higher pace of innovation and increasing investment in the restructuring the production apparatus, the energy system and the transport sector. This way we can set free a new economic dynamic, a long wave of environmentally friendly growth. In any case, the question of whether the world economy will continue to grow has long been decided. In view of the growing world population and the economic rise of the countries of the South, the all-important question is whether we will succeed in decoupling economic growth and environmental damage.

It is tempting to approach the ecological transformation as a master plan that specifies in detail which goals are to be achieved, how and by when. A highly complex industrial society interwoven with diverse external relations cannot be reconstructed like a building according to a preconceived plan.

There is no doubt that the ecological transformation needs an active, regulating and investing state that sets the course for private-sector initiatives. Investments worth billions in climate-friendly chemical plants and steel mills will only take place if companies can count on green electricity and hydrogen being available in large quantities and competitive prices. Overshooting operating costs compared to conventional processes must either be rewarded by the markets or compensated by tax breaks or other promotion schemes.

Governments should establish lead markets for climate-friendly key technologies and provide the necessary infrastructure like power grids and transport facilities for hydrogen. Smart market design can help.[2] But top-down control with tightly meshed state guidelines can never replace the innovative power of the market economy, which bundles the knowledge and initiative of millions and millions of producers and consumers.

To believe that we already know what the energy system, mobility and agriculture will look like in 2045 is to write the present into the future. The International Energy Agency estimates that about half of the necessary greenhouse

---

2 See Wambach, Achim: "Smart market design for sustainable infra-structures" in this volume.

gas reductions depend on innovations that are still in the research and development stage today. We neither know which innovative leaps the rapid technological development will lead to, nor can we predict the relative costs of different technology paths. A successful climate strategy must aim to set in motion a self-sustaining dynamic of ecological innovations and investments. It must combine ambitious goals with competition for the best solutions. And it must take into account reserves for economic bottlenecks and geopolitical conflicts. In times of political and economic turmoil, resilience is key.

Democracy is not negotiable

The criticism of the slowness and never-ending compromises of democracies has a long tradition. It is no coincidence that prominent environmentalists like Jorgen Randers from Norway sympathize with the Chinese model. If one understands the ecological turn primarily as a restriction of production and consumption, this is consistent. Then autocratic regimes are more likely to be able to enforce the necessary sacrifices. Democracy becomes a luxury that we can no longer afford in view of melting icebergs; freedom is reduced to the acceptance of ecological necessity.

For all the criticism of apocalyptic visions and authoritarian tendencies: Under no circumstances should liberals play down the dimension of the ecological crisis. If global warming gets out of control, this will result in major disasters, from economic collapse to global mass migration. In this respect, the environmental crisis also endangers democracy. We must therefore do everything possible to promote the ecological transformation without sacrificing civil liberties.

Those who want to reconcile freedom and ecology must above all focus on innovation and promote competition for the best solutions. Of course, even a liberal climate policy cannot do without limits and prohibitions. But they are not the best way to solve the ecological question. A liberal ecology policy focuses on incentives instead of restrictions. The most effective approach is the inclusion of ecological costs in market prices. A market economy only works if prices tell the ecological truth. EU emissions trading remains the key instrument of an ambitious European climate policy. To be economically viable, it is essential to win over as many partners as possible for an international CO_2 regime.

An ambitious European climate policy needs multilateral agreements that create comparable standards and competitive conditions. The additional burdens arising from environmental taxes can be compensated by reducing taxes on earned income and social security levies. Rising energy prices can be offset by a per capita flat rate, which also has a positive distributional effect in favour of lower incomes.

Decoupling prosperity and environmental degradation

Let us be clear about this: There is no freedom without responsibility. That is why it is ethically right to cycle or take the train and not to buy any products for which people are harmed or animals suffer. Everyone is free to seek the "good life" in more free time and rich social relations rather than in an increase in income and consumption. But a closer look at the size of the ecological challenge shows that it cannot be solved with an appeal for sufficiency. Without a profound green industrial revolution, we will not win the race against climate change. It requires a fundamental shift to renewable energies, a boost in resource efficiency and the transition to a modern circular economy. In essence, it is about decoupling the production of wealth from the consumption of nature. Although this is ambitious, it is feasible.

In view of the ecological stress limits of the Earth system, we are left with two almost unlimited sources of progress: the radiation of solar energy onto the Earth and human creativity. A sustainable civilization must be built on a combination of both. Those who pit ecology and freedom against each other will lose both in the end.

Europe has all the prerequisites to be a pioneer for a climate-neutral industrial society and a centre of competence for ecological innovation. Developing environmentally friendly, globally compatible solutions for the needs of a growing world population is our most important contribution in the fight against climate change. No one is interested in a progress-weary, future-anxious shrinking Europe. If we want to remain relevant, we must dare to set out on the path to ecological modernity.

II Liberal Answers to the Challenges of our Time

On the Critical Infrastructure of Liberal Democracy

Jan-Werner Müller

The topic of infrastructure is in fashion. Despite the Republicans' generally obstructionist attitude, Joe Biden has won cross-party support for his plan to have America's dilapidated bridges and collapse-prone tunnels repaired; in Germany, since the deficits in the pandemic have become so painfully clear, the digital infrastructure is finally being taken seriously. No one can find fault with this, as the general need is so obvious.

It is less clear that democratic politics also needs infrastructure – and that does not just mean polling stations that are easily accessible. In principle, infrastructure means: possibilities to reach and be reached by others; that is why road networks and even the post (mercilessly politicised by Trump, you may remember) are prime examples of infrastructure. And how about in a liberal, representative democracy? In this respect, it is necessary above all to have parties and professional media that enable citizens to connect with each other or, expressed in more abstract terms, to effectively use and unite their fundamental communicative political freedoms in order to unite. It was not without reason that the first German language weekly newspaper, which was published in the early 17th century in Strasbourg, bore the name *Relation*. Much-maligned social media sites are therefore not in themselves a threat to democracy – on the contrary. But it is important to regulate them in a pro-democratic way.

All this does not mean that more connectivity options alone can defuse threats to democracy. And they should certainly not to be attuned to the communitarian-kitschy choir (which is always particularly vocal in Germany), according to which democracy primarily means cohesion. The fact that there are connections and that people can easily reach others has long since not implied consensus or even solidarity. Motorways allow freedom of movement, they don't mean that we're all driving in one direction (or how many people you have as passengers in the car). Except: in a democracy, it is not at all a question of showing everyone the right direction. And just as the point of a journey does not derive from the existence of crash barriers, democracy is exhausted when drawing regulatory boundaries. But no one can deny that they perform an important function.

Effective use of fundamental political freedoms

Contrary to the proponents of "illiberal democracy", according to whom popular rule is reduced to the ballot box, democracy is unthinkable without the effective use of fundamental political rights such as freedom of expression, assembly and association (which are also restricted in one way or another by the illiberals in order to secure their power, without officially abolishing elections). The value of these communication rights increases significantly if organisations facilitate their use. I can also demonstrate on my own in the street, and send all my unpublished opinion articles to family and friends, or let them end up in the spam filters of strangers. But it is evident that political parties and the supposedly "old" media are especially capable of working miracles when it comes to disseminating a message (and so can other organisations, however; with the focus on parties and the press in the broadest sense, the value of civil society institutions or even trade unions should not be denied; although: representative democracy without parties and the press is not possible).

Certainly not everyone has such a rosy picture of "mediating institutions". Critics complain that organisations who, as it were, have pushed themselves between the people and the political system, have always reinforced inequality. Liberals such as Alexis de Tocqueville, one of the great advocates of the *corps intermédiaires* in the nineteenth century, have always been accused of having legitimised something like aristocracy by praising these entities in a roundabout way – an accusation that resonates even in today's contempt for "political class" or the "media bubble". There is no mediation at all, according to popular criticism, but instead the true voice of the people is distorted. Trump once described Twitter as a newspaper without losses, and on another occasion as a literary medium for which he has a unique talent (after all, with his usual modesty, he did name himself the "Ernest Hemingway of the 140 characters"). Above all, however, he declared Twitter to be his "megaphone" with which he could penetrate the supposed "noise" of the traditional elites. Beppe Grillo, founder of the Five Star Movement in Italy, urged supporters to make direct contact via his blog, thus avoiding the *casta* of corrupt politicians and professional journalists. The "ordinary people" knew best what the point really was; Grillo's promise was simply to function as their "amplifier".

It would be premature to call social media structurally populist on the basis of such (false) promises. In the first place, the question is: what exactly is the critical infrastructure of democracy supposed to achieve? On the one hand, it is intended to make it possible for citizens – including their conflicts – to represent society and to experience it. Opposites do not simply exist objectively; interests, ideas and, yes, identities must first be presented as politically relevant. In other words: it is not necessary to explain to workers that they are workers, but only a socialist party may make it plausible for them to be part of a working class which is at loggerheads with the owners of the means of production. That is why the popular talk in Germany of the "representation gap" is so misleading: representation claims are not simply there; they are formed by parties (and also by professional media focused on politics) – without anyone suspecting this process as being necessarily paternalistic or even manipulative.

In a democracy, it should be as easy as possible to make new offers of representation. This is especially true for parties whose job it is to start disputes and to settle conflicts in a productive way. But it is not forbidden for the media to launch campaigns to draw attention to grievances. Greats in the history of journalism such as the Briton W. T. Stead, one of the inventors of the interview and investigative research, was not wrong to see himself as a modern tribune of the people.

Productive – and unproductive – conflicts in democracy

From a democratic theory point of view, it is not decisive that everyone should always pay great attention to cohesion – if that were the only thing that mattered, it would perhaps always be best not to start any quarrels at all, however justified the reasons for them may be. What matters, rather, is that conflict participants do not suggest that their political opponents were not actually part of the people, or even that they were existential enemies – the classic manoeuvre of the authoritarian right-wing populists who, as is well known, always claim that only they represented the people, or what they also like to call the "true people". In accordance with this political logic, the following also applies: productive conflicts can only be fought with conflict partners who are recognised; however, those who do not belong at all cannot be partners from the outset.

Moreover, anyone who wants to wage democratic disputes must respect a minimum of facts. One thing is clear: "the facts" never speak for themselves, and the idea that facts and opinions can always be nicely and neatly separated is an illusion. Although the following also applies: anyone who does not recognise a common factual basis at all will not be able to perceive others as legitimate conflict partners. You can no longer reach anyone; and you become unreachable for others.

"Pluralism" may sound like a cliché from social studies – but it is crucial that a democracy does not lose its open, dynamic, indeed even creative character. There must be a variety of political and journalistic offerings – and, less obviously: ideally, mediating institutions should also be pluralistic within. The Basic Law even makes intra-party democracy a duty, and councils monitor the balance of the media.

To some, this may seem contradictory: after all, you join a party because you share very specific principles, not because you are endlessly pluralistically tolerant. And a readership wants a particular newspaper because they want to read contemporary affairs interpreted from a conservative perspective, for example. Except: no principle is implemented by itself, there must be constant discussions and weighing up; and a paper that always only delivers what is ideologically to be expected becomes a (boring) propaganda instrument. Without conflict, it is not possible.

What it means to completely abandon the claim to internal pluralism and the capacity for conflict can be demonstrated once again by an example from the USA. Trump, as is well known, transformed the Republican Party into a kind of personality cult: anyone who does not pay homage to the reality TV star, or even dares to claim that Biden legitimately won the 2020 election, is declared a traitor and is, in part, literally excluded from the Party. Without pluralism, there can be no critical loyalty or legitimate opposition within a party that could have reined in an authoritarian like Trump early enough. And, as is well known, there are hardly any people left in the Trump-loyal media who, committed to their journalistic conscience, would have insisted on facts.

Competition, rights, transparency – is that enough?

The problem with the Trumps and Grillos of this world is not that they make an offer of representation to potential supporters. The problem is simply that they claim that they are the only ones to represent the people and fundamentally deny legitimacy to all political opponents in the name of the people (which does not mean that the exclusion of certain actors could never be justified – the motto is militant democracy). Nor is the problem that addressing citizens is "direct". Firstly, "directness" is an illusion here; after all, it needs a medium like Twitter. And secondly, it is also perfectly acceptable that new political collectives arise on the Web. The danger is that the business model of some platforms – Facebook is the obvious example – rewards de facto hate campaigns and leads users with increasingly radical offerings to keep at it – that is, on the platform. The scientists Quinn Slobodian and William Callison coined the term *"incitement capitalism"*[1] to capture this dynamic (although, of course, there are also hate campaigns without private profit); Shoshana Zuboff points out that it is not technology in itself which dictates the constant monitoring of online behaviour for the purpose of generating advertising revenue.[2] The notion, popular with liberal observers in the broadest sense, that the irrational masses had brought the political disasters of Trump and Brexit upon themselves – and that more "gatekeepers" would be needed to keep the people out and keep them quiet – overlooks the fact that specific business elites are responsible for such business models, not "the mob". There would be nastiness even without the Internet; the fact that the haves find each other and that their nastiness is strengthened, or that new ways of being nasty are suggested to them – this is a matter of structures that could also be shaped differently.

In fact, social media would be an important extension of the infrastructure of democracy – they simply enable more *relations* (to recall once again the promise of the first German newspaper). The fear of them systematically reducing pluralism is known to be based on the idea that helpless people are being trapped in filter bubbles and locked up in echo chambers here. Recent research shows that the echo chamber theory has itself been repeatedly confirmed even in a kind of scientific echo chamber – but that it is empirically not necessarily plausible. If you think about it, you will quickly come to the conclusion that, in our offline life, we move about in quite homogeneous groups – but on the Internet, we are constantly finding completely different perspectives (to your own annoyance, as is often added). It should not be denied that there are

---

1 Slobodian, Quinn/Callison, William: "Coronapolitics from the Reichstag to the Capitol", in: Boston Review, January 12, 2021. https://bostonreview.net/articles/quinn-slobodian-toxic-politics-coronakspeticism/
2 Zuboff, Shoshana: The Age of Surveillance Capitalism. Frankfurt/New York: Campus 2018.

veritable waves of self-affirmation; but it does not yet follow that social media is in itself anti-pluralistic. The problem is that, unlike with parties and traditional news media, there is no diversity of providers.

Democratic digital infrastructure – part of the solution?

In addition, there are a number of important initiatives for democratic digital infrastructure, particularly public platforms, which do not follow the model of profit-by-surveillance-by-advertising. Analogous to the American Corporation for Public Broadcasting – public service television which, contrary to popular opinion, does exist in the United States, but only on a small scale – a Corporation for Public Software has been proposed. This would make apps freely available which should, above all, enable an open exchange among citizens. Once again, it would be naïve to think that a consensus would quickly emerge here: freedom of communication and communitisation, Armin Nassehi once said, are in fact mutually exclusive.[3] But freedom of communication, manipulated for profit, is still something special that could be regulated in a very different way.

Clever observers have repeatedly stressed that all this is perhaps not quite so easy. The approaches that are clear to everyone today – more competition instead of monopolies; more individual rights for users; more transparency – are based on basic ideas that liberals could have recited mechanically in the nineteenth century. This does not make these ideas wrong; however, whether they are sufficient to make a platform economy compatible with democracy or even to promote it is a legitimate question. This essay does not give a conclusive answer to this question; but it does illustrate what a critical infrastructure of liberal democracy is supposed to achieve in general.

---

3   Nassehi, Armin: Patterns. Theory of the Digital Society, Munich: C.H. Beck 2019.

Freedom in Times of the Pandemic

Sabine A. Döring

Whereas in Germany at the beginning of the pandemic the official measures to combat Covid were actively supported by a majority of people, since the autumn of 2020 we have been experiencing an increasingly vocal protest movement. Hate comments and calls for violence spread on the internet against the police, politics and science have increased enormously; there have even been physical attacks and torchlight marches in front of residential buildings. How should a liberal democracy deal with this? What lessons about freedom do we learn from the pandemic?

The virus is a challenge to liberal democracy

Our liberal democracy has been presented with a new challenge by the new SARS-CoV-2 virus. Political decision-making in dealing with the pandemic is characterised by an unprecedented combination of importance, the need for scientific expertise, uncertainty and utmost urgency. To put this in comparison to climate change: climate change is the more important problem in the medium and long term. Perceptions and responses to both problems are heavily influenced by scientific knowledge and advice. What the outcome will be if we implement the measures recommended by science can only be predicted with great uncertainty. However, with a spreading virus, every day (containment), every week (mitigation) or every month (vaccination rate) counts, whereas with climate change we calculate in years. This is because the processes underlying climate change are cumulative (although there are tipping points), whereas the spread of a virus is a multiplicative process.

Both crises call for collective action. First, individual action has consequences for others. While in climate change the individual CO_2 footprint adds up to a global emission, in the pandemic everyone can become a massive spreading factor. Second, there is a free-rider problem: a solution also benefits those who do not incur costs. Third, scientific expertise is essential to manage both crises because individuals cannot foresee what the global impact of their actions would be. This means, technically speaking, that a privately negotiated solution according to the Coase theorem is off the table. It is not possible without state intervention.[1]

An optimal intervention to slow climate change from a liberal perspective relies on market incentives, because it is about reduction: CO_2 is a by-product of highly valued goods such as electricity, heat or goods production. The goal is to reduce the sum of global emissions to a neutral balance. Scarcity through a Pigouvian tax or more efficiently still through certificates leaves the path to reduction to the market. It is difficult to find comparable starting points for measures in line with the market in a pandemic, especially since it is not a matter of reduction as in the case of CO_2, but of "elimination" in the sense of a low incidence strategy without availability of a vaccine and sustainable risk management until the endemic phase is reached with vaccines. For each individual, they must be prevented from becoming a link in a chain of infection. The best way to achieve this is through regulation, and that means general bans or mandates such as a contact ban, mandatory masking or, if the required vaccination rate cannot be achieved otherwise, mandatory vaccination. While the climate does not care who does the CO_2 reduction (it is the global total alone that counts), the elimination of a virus fails unless the privileged and the petulant also comply. This is the reason why epidemiologists attach such importance to the vaccination rate. Even if vaccination is not the only way out of the pandemic today, it is still the most important one.

Vaccination is morally imperative

Insofar as, first, the risks of vaccination are negligible compared to the risks of Covid-19 infection, and second, increasing the vaccination rate reduces the need for government restrictions on everyone, it is morally imperative to make one's solidarity contribution to the vaccination rate. No ethic worthy of the name provides a good reason why others should suffer from Covid-19 patients simply because they were so "free" not to get vaccinated when they could. It

---

1   Coase, Ronald H.: "The Problem of Social Cost", in: The Journal of Law & Economics 3 (1960).

does not follow, however, from the rightness of a moral duty to vaccinate that a legal duty to vaccinate is right: for liberals, the latter will be the ultima ratio. Conversely, however, it does not follow from the fact that a compulsory vaccination is not decided by law that we are not morally obliged to be vaccinated. Not everything that is permitted by law is morally right.

Like all disasters, Covid makes this visible as if under a burning glass. Catastrophes are the "moment of truth" insofar as they require solidarity-based action. Whereas in calmer times we can still get by if most of us pay our taxes, obey the traffic laws and otherwise mainly look after our own interests, Covid forces upon us the insight that people can unintentionally become a danger to others. To be sure, "negative externalities", that is, adverse effects of one's actions on others for which the actor does not account, have always played an important role in policy debates. Examples include debates about climate change, migration or the welfare state. But the coronavirus crisis probably makes us see these effects more clearly than ever before. Those who simply ignore the negative external effects of their own actions and refuse to take responsibility for them are acting "selfishly". The egoist does not make his own contribution to the common good, but at the same time builds on profiting in turn from the blessings of the common good. He is a "free-rider", no matter what his motives or reasons may be.

There is much more at stake than vaccination or Covid measures in general. Free-riders often argue under the guise of personal responsibility or freedom. Clearly, free-riding is precisely not personal responsibility. For in the genuine ordoliberal sense of the phrase, "personal responsibility" would mean paying for the damage caused to oneself and others by one's own actions or omissions. He who takes the benefit must also bear the damage, is how Walter Eucken begins his *Principles of Economic Policy*, published in 1952.[2] In any case, as has already been made clear, a pandemic – like climate change – cannot be combated by personal responsibility alone, as this requires coordinated action.

Free-riders cannot invoke freedom

Nor can the free-rider invoke the concept of freedom. Superficially, he emphasises the defence against illegitimate state intervention in individual options for action. He seems to be concerned with what Isaiah Berlin called "negative

---

2 Eucken, Walter: Grundsätze der Wirtschaftspolitik. Stuttgart: utb 2004.

freedom" as freedom from interference. People could and should decide for themselves what they really want. So far, so good. Except that freeloaders, unlike true liberals, underplay the fact that freedom is a normative concept. Negative freedom – or "republican freedom" as freedom from arbitrary rule, developed not least by Philip Pettit – is supposed to protect "positive freedom" as the freedom to self-determination.[3] Self-determination, however, does not mean "arbitrary freedom", i.e. unlimited satisfaction of arbitrary preferences, but autonomy as reasonable (or at least reflexive) self-determination. It is about protecting something that is worth protecting. Today, we would hardly want to protect the "freedom" to torture children. This aspect of the one, unitary freedom to be thought of becomes irrelevant in the face of the egoism of the free-rider. A widespread strategy in current political discourse is to protest reflexively and unreflectively at any state restriction of freedom (firecrackers or cheap meat, Covid measures or climate protection measures).

In the background, there is often an unwillingness to strain one's head in order to possibly have to leave one's comfort zone once insight has been gained. This strategy of declaring freedom to be a carte blanche for securing one's own privileges poses a fundamental danger to liberal democracy, which cannot rely on any relevant liberal thinker.

Freedom takes place within the framework of a community

Freedom, true liberals are clear about, always already takes place within the framework of a community and must be universalisable, i.e. apply to all, ideally within the framework of global society (in the debate about climate justice, even future generations are included). A liberal democracy therefore cannot avoid limiting individual freedom in favour of the freedom of all. The consensus in liberal democracy, with Isaiah Berlin, is that autonomy must not be understood as being determined "from the outside", at worst at the cost of the individual virtually disappearing in the community. No state or other power, claiming to know better than the limited individual what is worth protecting or striving for, may establish paternalism or authoritarianism – a tyranny of moralists. But the existence of this danger, on the other hand, cannot justify

---

3   Pettit, Philip: Just Freedom: A Moral Compass for a Complex World, W. W. Norton & Company, First Edition, 2014.

fundamental scepticism on the question of agreement on the limits of individual freedom within the framework of a liberal community. The liberal invokes the "fundamental liberal principle" formulated by John Stuart Mill and identified as such by Gerald Gaus, according to which the burden of proof is always borne by those who wish to limit individual freedom.[4] In many cases, however, it will be possible to provide this proof: trivially in the case of capital crimes, but certainly also in the case of many measures to combat pandemics. Fundamental rejection of any restriction of individual freedom would instead lead to anarchy in the form of a tyranny of the strong.

The question of which external effects should be internalised, where the boundary of the domain of responsibility for others – or solidarity – and the domain of personal responsibility runs, cannot be left to the individual. After all, what is at stake is the basic order or constitution we give ourselves as a community. Ideally, this question is answered in a continuous (ethically) informed social discourse of all free and equal people, in the course of which results are codified in each case within the framework of a democratic process. Without this order, the individual would be without orientation and protection in the community in which his actions necessarily take place. The law of the strongest would apply. Ideally, this order establishes solidary action in freedom instead.

This is not to say that individual conceptions would converge on a single "true" theory of the good. From the point of view of our liberal democracy, such a perfectionist theory of the good is outdated and even dangerous: religious, cultural or political ideas that promise a single truth will not be feasible in a just society of free and equal citizens simply because of the "burdens of judgment" (John Rawls) and have too often entailed too much cruelty. Nonetheless, our participation as citizens in the social community requires us to do at least "what we owe to each other" (in terms of justice).[5] Therefore, instead of blindly indulging in limitless pleasure, we will have to critically examine every possible source of happiness for its externalities. Here again Mill has a point when he argues against Jeremy Bentham's purely quantitative hedonism for a qualitative hedonism, declaring that it is "better to be Socrates dissatisfied than a fool satisfied".[6] The contented Socrates and true liberal will take facts and arguments

---

4   Gaus, Gerald: Justificatory Liberalism: An Essay on Epistemology and Political Theory, Oxford: University Press 1996.
5   Scanlon, Thomas M.: What We Owe to Each Other, Cambridge: Harvard University Press 2000.
6   Mill, John S.: Utilitarianism. London: Parker, Son and Bourn 1863.

into account without letting them spoil his fun. On the other hand, that attitude in the political sphere which Quassim Cassam has christened "epistemic carelessness" and which in the end leads to "bullshit" has nothing to do with liberalism.[7]

We need solidarity and tolerance

All of this presupposes the mutual fulfilment of certain normative expectations, both of citizens towards each other and of the state towards its citizens and citizens towards the state, for this is the necessary condition for mutual respect and mutual trust and thus the indispensable basis of solidarity and tolerance. In a pluralistic society, this path is not a loss of freedom, but its condition, insofar as an agreement between free and equal can only succeed in this way. Like the victory over the virus, agreement in a pluralistic society can only succeed if everyone thinks along with the others and no one "crosses the line", i.e. if everyone is not simply left to do their own thing.

Liberalism will nevertheless distinguish itself from other conceptions of what is politically correct by declaring freedom to be a fundamental political value and, for this very reason, by invoking the fundamental liberal principle. Reconciling this value and this principle in their content and their practical implementation with the recognition of state regulation under conditions to be specified in each case will be the defining project of the future for our self-determination, our regulation of feelings, our concepts of the good life and our living together – not only in times of pandemic.

---

7   Cassam, Quassim: "Vice Epistemology", in: The Monist 99:2 (2016), S. 159–180.

Liberalism versus Right-Wing Populism

Sabine Leutheusser-Schnarrenberger

"One loves only what sets one free" (Friedrich Schiller). Hardly any sentence could better express the longing of many people after more than two years of pandemic.

Addressing the future of liberalism today should actually be quite easy. Never before have there been so many restrictions on liberty in peacetime as during the coronavirus pandemic, never before have people ruled by decree for so long and made parliament a fence-sitter. Never have schools been closed for so long and universities deserted. And never before has there been such an insistent fight for compulsory vaccination. Compulsory vaccination for everyone over the age of 18 – this in Germany, where the Federal Constitutional Court has derived the right to be sick from the fundamental rights of physical integrity and general freedom of action, of self-determination. That would have been unimaginable a few years ago.

In this exceptional situation, in which the state had a responsibility as a risk manager that it sometimes fulfilled well, sometimes poorly; in this time, in which the political failures of earlier years became mercilessly visible – for example, the inadequate digital infrastructure in schools and health offices; in this time, the conditions should be ideal for a strengthening liberalism, which powerfully relies on the freedom of the individual, in the spirit of Friedrich Schiller. Standing up for freedom even in times of a pandemic should be a matter of course for liberals. Liberalism is based on an image of man who, guided by reason, should be able to develop freely and live up to his responsibility in a plural society. "We are born free in order to be free", as Hannah Arendt put it.[1]

Freedom, however, is not something absolute. Freedom is a regulative idea, and regulative ideas are always situation- and time-bound. Therefore, it is generally not a problem that the limits of freedom are always being renegotiated.

---

1   The Freedom to Be Free: Hannah Arendt, Penguin 2020.

However, if freedom is no longer understood as something that belongs to the individual, but to society as a whole, then this is a fundamental paradigm shift. The experience of the history of two dictatorships has shown us Germans in particular how important it is to link the concept of freedom and dignity to the individual. If the concepts of freedom and dignity were now to be decoupled from the individual and transferred to a collective, this would be associated with great dangers. The concerns and legitimate interests of the individual would have to take a back seat to an asserted general good of society. This basic attitude characterises populism from both the right and the left. Liberals should not adopt it as their own.

Right-wing populism is about the freedom of the collective

Right-wing populism propagates the absolute freedom of the collective. The people, which are set as homogeneous, are to be free from everything that does not serve the implementation of their common will. This would also satisfy the need for personal freedom, because in the homogeneous community the individual will is suspended in the common will. With reference to actual or supposed grievances, the social elites are held responsible as antagonists of the people, indeed as traitors to the people. For this purpose, an "ideological minimum" is sufficient, which is not coincidentally reminiscent of Carl Schmitt's thinking. It stems from an idea according to which politics is generated solely from the antagonism of friend and foe.

We are dealing here with a conception of politics based on an ethnically homogeneous body of the people, whose task is to protect the own from the foreign, the us from the other, and the people from the elites. Politics is understood as a cathartic process serving to purify the self from all that is foreign, through which only the true will, the common will of the homogeneous people, the *volonté générale*, is brought to bear.

The political thrust of right-wing populism and the danger it poses to our free democratic order can be made particularly clear by referring to Carl Schmitt. For it is not only the understanding of politics based on exclusion, but also the contempt for the German Basic Law together with the constitutional thinking that set in after the end of the Second World War that links today's right-wing populism with Carl Schmitt's thinking. With the same arrogance and obtuseness with which Carl Schmitt exulted in 1933 in the face of Adolf Hitler's assumption of power, that now at last "the remnants of the (hated) liberal-democratic system are sinking more and more", he believed that in his post-war publications he could deride the advocates of the Basic Law as "constitutionalists" and mock the Basic Rights of the Basic Law as "inalienable donkey rights".

Freeing the peoples from the prison of liberal democratic constitutions, freeing the Germans from the prison of the Basic Law, is precisely where right-wing populism sees its historically legitimised mission. Right-wing populism radically opposes all those precautions which the authors of the more recent constitutions in Europe and which the parents of the Basic Law provided in 1949 as safeguards against a renewed slide into the unjust state.

This conception of the state, the exaltation of the German people and the political conception designed to exclude everything that is not German is a declaration of war on liberalism. The authoritarianism sought by right-wing populists aims at weakening institutions of the democratic rule of law and public criticism – parliaments, opposition parties, independent courts and free media.

Liberalism must oppose right-wing populism

Liberalism must oppose this destructive right-wing populism with all its might. There must be no uncertainty and no despondency. That is one of its greatest tasks today.

From the great philosophical ideas of political life, with its origins in the Enlightenment of the 17th and 18th centuries, in the *Vormärz* of the 19th century, and its transformations in the 20th century, have emerged the right to political participation, the principle of self-development and self-determination, the rights of freedom enforceable by the means of the rule of law, and economic independence in a society free of discrimination. They are central elements of liberalism.

For liberals, freedom is first of all a foregone conclusion. They subject decisions to a freedom compatibility test. According to this understanding, restrictions are the last resort. The freedom of one necessarily restricts the freedom of another. These interactions make constant trade-offs necessary, as do tensions with other state goals such as domestic security. These are precisely the frictions we are experiencing in the pandemic. The viability of the state's healthcare system is being used to justify massive, albeit temporary, restrictions on liberty. In many cases, in view of the health risks to particularly vulnerable people, the encroachments on freedom are judged to be proportionate – even by the courts.

Threats to freedom

Political liberalism today is challenged by the deep fissures in our society, by the rawness and radicalisation of communication, by social media as hatemongers, by cancel culture with its threat to academic freedom, and by identity politics that promote exclusion. In these developments lie great dangers for the self-determination of the individual, who may no longer dare to participate in the discourse and struggle for the right solutions that are so essential for democracy. Hatred and incitement against politicians can become a danger to our representative democracy. The pandemic has driven people to protest, which is fundamentally legitimate, but which becomes dangerous when it is instrumentalised by others, as is the case with the far right.

That freedom is a defining value of liberalism needs no explanation. But some people may not understand that it is not to be understood with the absolute claim of assertion at any price. They shorten the concept of freedom by not understanding responsibility as necessarily connected with freedom. Responsibility for oneself, but in a civil society also for the other, also for the future of future generations.

In its fundamental decision on climate protection, the Federal Constitutional Court elaborated precisely this responsibility.[2] In order to safeguard freedom secured by fundamental rights, the legislature would have had to take precautions to mitigate the high burdens caused by emissions. A freedom-preserving transition to climate neutrality would have to be guaranteed. Thus, the obligations arising from the state objective of environmental protection in Article 20a of the Basic Law also have an effect on the right to freedom of future generations.

Part of liberalism, then, is that the state should interfere as little as necessary with liberties, but equally that the state should not become too high-handed. For liberalism, state restraint is an intrinsic component. But a one-

---

2 Vgl. The Federal Constitutional Court: To the Order of the First Senate of 24 March 2021 (Climate Change). https://www.bundesverfassungsgericht.de/SharedDocs/Entscheidungen/EN/2021/03/rs20210324_1bvr265618en.html

sided focus against the state, which sees in every suggested restriction a disproportionate encroachment and in every binding requirement the authorisation to denounce, is no service to freedom and certainly no proof of courageous thinking. The struggle over the tasks and the necessary action of the state are permanent challenges that liberalism cannot avoid.

With the pandemic and the initially central role of the state as actor and manager, parts of the population have become accustomed to the restrictions and to a state that has taken the reins of action – at times even without parliamentary scrutiny. Surveys have shown this. This need not give rise to too much concern if this attitude is not maintained after the end of the pandemic. But if the special pandemic situation turns into the "new" normality with the state as the general problem solver for as many issues as possible, there is cause for concern. And if a fundamentally different understanding of liberal democracy were to develop from this, then there is justified cause for great concern.

Freedom or full protection

It is not only in times of pandemics that the need for the most comprehensive coverage possible stands in direct opposition to a liberal mindset. We must not become accustomed to deep encroachments on fundamental rights, because this can lead to a development in which state powers are overstretched, the indispensable balancing of conflicting fundamental rights is no longer carried out at all, and ultimately constitutional fundamental rights exist only on paper.

The image of man in the Basic Law – characterised by dignity, reason, self-determination in all situations – would no longer correspond to political reality. The postulate of freedom could then be reduced to economics. Unrestrained market mechanisms would be confronted with patronised citizens. The result would be the divisibility of liberties – entrepreneurial freedom, professional self-realisation and largely uninhibited economic development opportunities would be juxtaposed with the limitation of freedom of expression, the restriction of the inconvenient right to demonstrate and an integration policy based purely on utilitarian considerations. Such a truncated understanding of liberalism bears authoritarian traits and contradicts the holistic claim to freedom. It is possible to see where this tendency has led in other European member states. The already contradictory term "illiberal democracy" conceals a deformed democracy that is not based on the principles of equal rights, the protection of minorities, the independence of the judiciary and uncontrolled journalists and independent media. These institutions, which are essential to a liberal democracy, are subordinated to the political will of those in power, and the opposition is hindered in its rights. However, the substantive rule of law with independent judges is an indispensable part of liberalism. The state must guarantee its ability to function.

Liberalism is characterised by open and level-headed debate on the major issues of our society: analysing, questioning, reflecting and discussing instead of denouncing, insulting, manipulating and turning facts into fakes – that is liberalism's claim on responsible citizens. The boundaries to criminal insult, incitement of the people and incitement to racial hatred must not be crossed, just as they must not be crossed to the threat of violence or its use. Of course, freedom of expression and the protection of personality must be brought into the right balance. But freedom does not just mean "I want" or "I don't want". No attitude is further from enlightened liberality than persisting in the pseudo-autonomous defiant phase of "I want to, but ...", the *Struwwelpeter*-like revolt against any form of necessary insight and higher power of judgment. The courage to use one's own intellect, as it corresponds to the Enlightenment, therefore proves itself not least in recognising one's own limits of judgment.[3]

Freedom cannot be understood only intellectually. The desire to express oneself, to live one's life, to have contact with other people, runs deep in people. If this freedom is drastically restricted, it can make people ill. We also experience this in the pandemic: there is the illness caused by the virus. But the lack of freedom also makes people sick – in a different way. We see this in the child psychiatric clinics, which are overflowing; we notice it in the cries for help from social psychological institutions.

The enemy of a politics of freedom is rigidity in fear and anxiety about the loss of vitality and about the future. The challenging task of political liberalism is to find a way between the false promise of unanimity, which denies social conflicts, and the equally false radical individualism.

---

3 Eilenberger, Wolfram: »Wir brauchen eine neue Aufklärung«, in: liberal 1 (2022).

Ownership for All! From Class Society to Property Society

Ralf Fücks

We are living in a period of rapid change. The global division of labour is changing in the course of globalisation, and traditional industries are coming under ever greater pressure. Digitalisation is changing the world of work like no other development before it. It is taking over a large part of today's activities. Outdated professions are disappearing, new ones are emerging. The transition to a post-fossil, climate-neutral economy is intensifying this upheaval. No stone is being left unturned in the energy industry, and the automotive sector and energy-intensive industries are on the verge of massive change.

The rise and fall of entire industries is not new. It accompanies the history of industrial societies. What is new, however, is that structural change is affecting a large part of the economy at the same time and is taking place at high speed. Digitalisation and globalisation open up new opportunities for the resourceful, energetic and well-qualified. At the same time, rapid change creates a fundamental sense of growing insecurity. What seemed secure yesterday can be completely different tomorrow. It is not surprising that part of society feels the loss of security more strongly than the opportunities that come with the new.

The polarisation between winners and losers of structural change and the sense of growing insecurity are a welcome sounding board for the anti-liberal revolt we have seen in Western democracies in recent years. Its most striking expression has been Donald Trump's presidency and the rise of right-wing populist parties in European democracies. The anti-liberal wave may have passed its peak, but the tendency towards growing polarisation and radicalisation is by no means broken. When globalisation, technological change and increasingly heterogeneous societies are perceived as a threat by a considerable part of society, the ground remains fertile for nationalist and xenophobic movements. Liberal democracies must therefore convey *security in times of change*.[1]

Societies need security in times of change

A minimum of stability in the living environment is needed if large sections of the population are not to perceive economic and social change as a threat to be averted. Security in times of change arises from a variety of factors, which are detailed in the final report of the expert commission "Security in Change" by the Center for Liberal Modernity in 2019. The commission developed 55 policy proposals in the areas of empowerment, internal security, civil society and social participation.[2] One central proposal shows that *private property* acts as a risk buffer for the changes in the world. Those who have their own home and certain financial reserves will face situations of change with more confidence and have more personal options.

Private property makes people independent and therefore freer. It is the economic basis of a self-confident civil society. At the same time, it is the foundation of a free economic order, which is essentially shaped by the individual responsibility of a large number of producers and consumers. The motto of a free society must not be the concentration of economic power in the hands of the state, but *ownership for all*.

The attitude that property is one of the basic democratic rights is not very widespread in Germany. Private wealth is considered suspect by many. "The millionaires" is a pejorative fighting term, and much of the political debate revolves around redistribution issues. A typical example is housing policy. In large parts of politics and the population, it is not the increased promotion of housing construction and home ownership, but strict state control that is seen as the cure for housing shortages and rising rents.

---

1   Center for Liberal Modernity: Security in Times of Change. Press Release, May 2019. https://libmod.de/en/report-security-in-times-of-change/
2   Ibid.

Property and the common good

"Property obliges" is one of the most quoted maxims of the German Basic Law. Article 14, paragraph 2 states: *"Property obliges. Its use shall at the same time serve the common good."* The concept of property in the Basic Law is opposed both to an unlimited absolutisation of private property and to the unbridled grip of politics. Encroachments on private property rights are bound to narrow conditions and must be compensated.

However, the Basic Law's commitment to private property is much more muted than in the classic documents of the bourgeois revolutions in the late 18th century. The French Declaration of the Rights of Man and of the Citizen of 1789, for example, states in Article 2: "The purpose of every political association is the preservation of the natural and inviolable rights of man. These are the right to liberty, the right to property, the right to security and the right to resist oppression."

Who today would still courageously include the right to property among the inalienable human rights and mention it in the same breath as the right to freedom? For the great thinkers of modern democracy – Locke, Montesquieu, Adam Smith – this connection was clear. For them, there is no civil liberty without the right to property. Property is the material basis for the self-responsibility of citizens. Its guarantee sets limits on the access of the state as well as on the arbitrariness of the rich and powerful, who cannot simply take what they like. Property makes self-care possible, i.e. the self-responsible shaping of the individual's life; it is a premium on professional success and thus strengthens the achievement principle. Private property does not necessarily have to manifest itself as individual ownership. Participation in common property – whether in cooperative form or as a shareholder in a large company – also falls under the category of private property, as long as it can be disposed of individually or according to jointly agreed rules.

At the same time, the acquisition and increase of private property is tied to social conditions that make it possible in the first place. First and foremost is the rule of law. Without it, there is no security of property. An efficient public infrastructure – transport, communications, education and science – also provides a foundation for private property accumulation. The success of private economic activity depends not only on the initiative and efficiency of the individual but also on public goods. For this reason, the maxim "property obliges" is not merely an imperative of social solidarity, but reflects the social conditionality of private property.

After all, property can only thrive in the long run if there is social peace in a society. The social acceptance of private property is tied to the fact that a society is reasonably just. Crass contrasts between the rich and the poor undermine the legitimacy of private property. It must not be a privilege of a small class of rich people. In this respect, it is precisely advocates of private property who should be concerned about the growing concentration of wealth in the hands of the few.

Skewed wealth distribution

According to a study by the German Institute for Economic Research (DIW), five per cent of the German population have 55 per cent of the total wealth.[3] The top one per cent has a good third of the national wealth, the top 0.1 per cent an impressive 20 per cent. The richest 45 households in the country own 4.7 per cent of the national wealth – about as much as the entire poorer half of the population.[4] Wealth inequality is passed on from generation to generation – ten per cent of the younger generation accounts for 50 per cent of inherited wealth. Inheritance tax dampens this effect, but does not compensate for it.

While income distribution has remained reasonably stable within the last decade, contrary to perceived public perception, the gap between the wealthy and those who have nothing has widened. This creates a structural inequality of opportunity and power that is incompatible with the social market economy. Private wealth is not only a buffer against the vagaries of life and a resource of civic autonomy, but in many cases it also provides access to the networks of power, information and contacts that are not available to poorer sections of the population.

The stock market and real estate boom fuelled by the ECB's zero interest rate policy has inflated assets – those who have will be given, those who have to live on their salary alone cannot make big leaps. The digital revolution will further accelerate the unequal development. Automation and artificial intelligence tend to replace labour with capital. This brings into focus the question of

---

3 DIW Berlin: »MillionärInnen unter dem Mikroskop: Datenlücke bei sehr hohen Vermögen geschlossen – Konzentration höher als bisher ausgewiesen«, in: DIW Wochenbericht 29 (2020), S. 511–521.

4 Bach, Stefan; Thiemann, Andreas & Zucco, Aline: Discussion Papers: Looking for the Missing Rich: Tracing the Top Tail of the Wealth, DIW Berlin 2018.

who will benefit from the digital dividend in the future: who owns the robots?[5] The imbalance in the distribution of wealth is exacerbated by the different taxation of labour and capital income.

It must be said, however, that the DIW study does not include pension entitlements. This distorts the statistics in favour of capital owners. Self-employed people have to build up private assets for their old-age provision, while employees and civil servants acquire individual claims to collective assets. Those who have a well-funded pension are often better off in old age than small-business owners or freelancers who have to live off their capital.

In Germany in particular, with its medium-sized economic structure, large fortunes are tied up in family businesses that employ millions of people and pay taxes locally. Their wealth therefore definitely benefits the common good.

Distributive justice is what counts

Both should be considered before hyperventilating in view of the figures quoted. Nevertheless, the imbalance in wealth distribution remains a fact that cannot be shrugged off. It undermines equal opportunities, creates separate worlds of life that hardly come into contact with each other, and inflates the speculative financial sector.

Capital incomes tend to rise more than wages and salaries as a result of globalisation and digitalisation. Therefore, strong wealth inequality also increases income inequality in the long run. There is some evidence that the concentration of disposable assets at the upper end of society dampens economic growth dynamics. In addition, there is a political-psychological aspect that should not be underestimated: if the majority of citizens have the impression that things are no longer fair, this destroys the legitimacy of a free economic order.

The social market economy is based on the promise of "prosperity for all". When a large part of the people who work every day are left behind while the rich get richer, it is grist to the mill for populist parties on both the left and the right. These are all reasons why a more balanced distribution of wealth needs to be addressed politically.

---

5   Südekum, Jens: »Digitalisierung und die Zukunft der Arbeit: Wem gehören die Roboter?«, in: IZA Newsroom August 7, 2018.

Those who see the reintroduction of wealth tax as the ideal way to achieve greater distributive justice are, however, thinking too briefly. If wealth taxes are to have a significant distributional effect, they must be set at such a high level that they severely interfere with business assets and attack the retirement provisions of the self-employed. Both are counterproductive in terms of economic and social policy. At the same time, wealth taxation only addresses the symptoms instead of tackling the cause of the problem: the lack of wealth accumulation among broad sections of the population.

The key to wealth distribution is participation in productive capital and real estate stock. The dividing line in wealth distribution runs between the strata who own shares in companies and attractive real estate and those who rely solely on their current incomes. Those who want to narrow the gap between the "bottom" and the "top" must put ownership of companies and real estate on a broader basis. Not "abolition of property" but "property for all" is the liberal answer to the property question.

Encourage capital formation

How can the private property accumulation of workers and employees be promoted? On the one hand, through higher net incomes that also enable higher savings. A flattening of the "cold progression" in wage and income tax would already help here.

At the same time, the acquisition of shares and real estate should be more strongly promoted for lower- and middle-income groups. A significant increase in the corresponding tax allowances is overdue. Another variant is to supplement the statutory pension with a funded pension component (equity pension) – either as a supplementary pillar or by investing part of the statutory pension contributions in private or state equity-based pension funds. Sweden has successfully introduced the model of a sovereign wealth fund; Germany's coalition agreement 2021 promises an entry into this model.

Employers and trade unions can also do more, for example by expanding capital-forming benefits as part of wage increases. In this way, part of the agreed wage increases could flow into inter-company funds that invest primarily in domestic companies. In the long term, this would exponentially increase the share of national wealth held by broad sections of the population.

Employee participation can also be expanded. When workers and employees become co-owners, it strengthens their identification with the company.

This is an untapped potential to improve the capital base of start-ups and medium-sized companies alike and to retain talented employees.

Last but not least, it is important to provide the best possible education for as many people as possible. In a knowledge society, general education and vocational qualifications are the most important "productive assets". They are the key to professional success, income and social participation. Therefore, investments in the public education system are also a contribution to a fairer society. Participatory justice is not only conveyed through private income and wealth, but also through public institutions (see the last article in this volume).

The advocates of liberal democracy must not leave the debate on distributive justice to their opponents. Not every debate on distribution is driven by pure envy and socialist egalitarianism. Equality of opportunity and social permeability are rather the foundations of a liberal democratic order.

Equity in performance, equal opportunities and upward social mobility are basic elements of a social democracy. At the same time, they are conditions of a dynamic economy. This also includes the broadest possible distribution of wealth. Those who want to make democracy and the market economy fit for the future should advocate an active wealth policy that makes as many citizens as possible economic participants.

Liberal Democracies versus Totalitarian Autocracies: European Responses to the Systemic Conflict

Daniela Schwarzer

Since 24th February 2022, Vladimir Putin's war has not only been shaking Ukraine, it has shaken Europe and the world. Thousands of civilians are falling victim to it, and millions are being forced to flee. It is a war against commitment and progress in a democratic state that has turned towards the Western liberal world.

Russia's President is trying to wipe out this country as a sovereign state with a right to self-determination, to defence and to the inviolability of its territory, based on an ethno-nationalist identity discourse that sees Ukraine and Belarus as part of Russia. For Vladimir Putin, the existence of this functioning democracy, with all the weaknesses that the system still has, is a problem. Inside Russia, in fact, where he is clinging to power and where only his truth is still allowed to exist in a public sphere which has been brought into line. Alternative points of view, a diversity of opinion and debates have long since lost their place in a totalitarian system that does not allow alternative public spheres to exist alongside Putin's.

The importance of the war in Ukraine extends far beyond the country. It is about peace and democracy on the European continent. It is an attack on Europe as part of an international order that respects national sovereignty and borders just as much as multilateral institutions, and in which war is not a politically legitimate means. In this respect, Ukraine profoundly defends European values and concepts of order – and, to the extent that the political West is not joining in the fight quickly and decisively for them, it is a threat not only to Ukraine, but to Europe and the rule-based international order.

The systemic conflict is complex

Russia's war in Ukraine can also be seen as the latest and most brutal form of an increasingly acute systemic conflict between liberal democracies and authoritarian regimes. China's ostensibly neutral stance on the conflict can be assessed in the same way.

For years, this systemic conflict has been reflected in less conspicuous but also consequential forms of political debate. It is being played out between liberal-democratic and authoritarian positions in the struggle for the future of our international order, which was largely created by the USA after the Second World War and which for a long time largely corresponded to Western concepts of order. For years, China has been trying to steer the international order away from its long-standing universal norms and principles, such as international law and human rights, through monetary and human resources policies, exerting political influence over decisions, blocking the very same, or perhaps creating alternative regional organisations such as the Asian Infrastructure Investment Bank (AIIB).

Moreover, the conflict between liberal democracies and authoritarian regimes is reflected in targeted interventions in other states. With disinformation campaigns, cyber attacks, economic pressure, and other forms of hybrid warfare, China and Russia, but also other players such as Turkey and Iran, are trying to intervene in Western states. In return, the activities of Western non-governmental organisations, foundations and other protagonists are also considered to be a manifestation of the systemic conflict, so that China or Russia ban them from their countries as "foreign agents" or no longer grant their employees an entry permit. As a result, relations between states that are in systemic competition with one another are becoming increasingly thin. Since social, scientific and cultural exchanges have become many times more difficult, there are often only government relations and business contacts behind which, however, when it comes to authoritarian regimes, the state is also at the forefront.

Liberal democracies are no longer seen as having no alternative

A third dimension of the systemic conflict has become particularly important as a result of the COVID-19 pandemic: The performance of the respective systems in combating the virus and its extensive consequences for the economy and society attracted attention. Discussions about the fact that authoritarian regimes were (if only ostensibly) more successful in fighting the pandemic have also aroused critics in the political West who doubt the ability of democracies to act. Time and again, it is said that only strictly hierarchical systems with the power to impose crackdowns are able to effectively end pandemics. Even with regard to the fight against climate change and its consequences, there are voices which consider democratic decision-making to be too long-winded, unfocused and too weak to enforce policies. The liberal credo that democracies are best able to overcome crises through creative solutions and innovations, and to stick together during such times, is thus called into question.

Thus, the situation in 2022 is markedly different from that in 1989, when the Cold War brought about the collapse of systemic competition between socialism and capitalism: There are now examples of political systems that are fundamentally different and yet successful. Liberal democracies and their once universally accepted value base are no longer seen as having no alternative.

Democratic systems – and that includes the European Union, as a supranational community of 27 members – must re-establish themselves and work to improve their performance capacity. Because, in view of their internal and external openness, they are particularly vulnerable by transnational threats and new forms of confrontation, including external interventions by means of hybrid warfare.

Responding to new challenges

The view that political systems must 'deliver' in order to maintain their legitimacy focuses on the question of what challenges our liberal democracies will have to face in the future if the process and opportunities for participation do not in themselves guarantee sufficient legitimacy. The list of topics is long at the beginning of the 2020s, because challenges within our political systems, our societies and our economic models are merged with global, transnational risks and tasks of unprecedented magnitude. For example, liberal democracies must find responses to climate change and its consequences, shape the digital revolution, and find increasing transnational migration and the growing inequalities in our societies.

Not only Russia's war in Europe, the rise of a technology-based authoritarian China, which supports autocrats worldwide and those who want to become autocrats, the realignment of the USA towards Asia, and the EU's relative loss in importance with regard to the economy, defence and demographics, are all changing the way Europeans perceive international opportunities and threats. Their attention is increasingly focused on how they can jointly develop the capacity to act in a world affected by crisis and conflict. Particularly in the case of states as deeply integrated as is the reality in the EU, the separation between internal and external challenges must be seen as outdated.

Today, it is no longer just a question of anticipating and averting threats. Knowing our vulnerability, the aim must be to increase the resilience of infrastructure, the economy and society, i.e. to ensure that a system, an organisation or even individuals can recover as quickly as possible from shocks and return to a functioning state, rather than collapse. Uncertainty has become the norm; disruptions and disasters must be expected. In particular, cyber attacks can have a massive impact on the security of the population and the ability of civil infrastructure to function.

Debates on the question of how it is possible to renew liberalism in an increasingly uncertain world are often confined to the national sphere. The EU belongs here – and this is not a problem, but a possible solution area.

Europe as a liberal project

The European Union and its Member States have been building on liberal principles since its inception: Liberalism has promoted democracy and the rule of law, free trade and an active civil society. At its core is the postulate of equal freedom for all, the normative idea of human rights and an international legal order. In short, liberalism has brought about democracy as we know it today. It has become so deep-rooted that we in the EU have long since used the terms "liberal democracy" and "democracy" almost interchangeably.

This shared understanding of values is firmly anchored in the Union by the Lisbon Treaty: The values on which the Union is founded are respect for human dignity, freedom, democracy, equality, the rule of law and the safeguarding of human rights, including the rights of those who belong to minorities. These values are common to a society characterised by pluralism, non-discrimination, tolerance, justice, solidarity and equality between women and men.

As in the liberal political constitution, liberalism is an integral part of the European market economy as the economic basis of an open society. The European Union is particularly committed to liberal openness: it is based on market integration, which should not only ensure prosperity, but also the free movement of goods, services, labour and capital.

The threat to European liberalism

Today, liberalism, understood as a broad, non-partisan way of political thinking, is also on the defensive in the European Union. The retrogression of national democracies is particularly worrying. Since 2010, right-wing populist Viktor Orbán has restricted the separation of powers, the independence of the judiciary and the freedom of the media and science to such an extent that the non-governmental organisation Freedom House no longer categorises the Hungarian state as a democracy. Since 2018, Hungary has been in the process of reviewing compliance with democratic principles and the rule of law under Article 7 of the EU Treaty.

Such proceedings are also under way against Poland. Particularly problematic is a judicial reform through which the ruling party can exert political influence over the two most important entities of the judicial system, judges and public prosecutors, and repeated disrespect of judgements of the European Court of Justice. Poland is not regarded by Freedom House as a functioning democracy any longer either. In the V-Dem Democracy Index, it ranks at number 80, even below Kosovo, Colombia and Georgia. Hungary is in an even worse position at number 91.

These developments are being intensified from the outside. Systemic competition between authoritarian regimes and democracies now extends deep within the EU. Through targeted disinformation and the promotion of anti-democratic forces, Russia and China, for example, undermine the stability of our systems. Cyberattacks and data theft are strategically used before elections to influence the results. China's long-term investment in exerting influence, for example through funding university chairs, think tanks and NGOs in Europe, is rightly being increasingly monitored.

Europeans, however, are far from being merely passive victims of undemocratic forces. Politicians and political parties are specifically seeking cooperation. China has become an important investor for many governments – often due to a lack of European alternatives. The fact that this is accompanied by the exertion of political influence has only changed the approach in some countries. The high price of the collaborations, which are interesting from an economic point of view, can be seen in the openly disclosed methods with which the Chinese Communist Party garners support. Particularly shocking for many Europeans was the realisation that US President Donald Trump and his team, in office from 2016 to 2020, became partners of anti-democratic and anti-European forces in the EU.

Democracy and the rule of law are fundamental principles of the EU to which each member state subscribed upon accession. In the first 50 years of integration, it was hardly conceivable for a state to move so far away from the need for sanction mechanisms to ensure their compliance. The fact that national governments, and also the EU institutions, have remained silent on the undermining of these principles for so long was a huge mistake. For the response to the dismantling of democracy and the rule of law must also be a political one. With Article 7 of the EU Treaty and the conditionality of EU funding, the EU now has two mechanisms at its disposal with which to defend the rule of law. They must be applied consistently with the full political support of governments. In addition, unfortunately, care must now also be taken in the EU to ensure that national and regional elections are conducted properly. In addition to the Organisation for Security and Co-operation in Europe (OSCE), civil society groups can play an important role in this.

A European agenda for the future

In order to protect the fundamental values of the European Union and the democracies that have merged within it, the Union must, as far as possible, be united, modernised and strengthened internally, because only greater resilience, competitiveness and capacity to act can ensure that we are able to assert ourselves as democracies with open societies in an increasing systemic conflict.

As a unique amalgamation of Western liberal democracies which has managed to secure peace, freedom and prosperity for over six decades and has a successful, integrated economy, which is today the most important export market for the USA, Russia or China, the EU can and must expand its international role. Together with like-minded partners around the world who share our values, Europeans should define a future agenda to counteract illiberal and authoritarian forces. For the EU, the aim should be to protect peace, prosperity, democracy and self-determined trade – in short: our Western liberal way of life.

The EU has been in crisis-combating mode for most of the last decade and survived the global financial crisis, the Euro crisis and the refugee crisis in the years before the global pandemic. The COVID-19 pandemic has shaken the European Union, but has also triggered an unprecedented level of cooperation and – perhaps most importantly – a new way of acting together. The EU has also reacted to Putin's war in Ukraine in a united way.

The war on our continent, the disintegration of the European security order and the deepening of the systemic conflict, are presenting Europe with new, common tasks that make even clearer what the financial crisis or even the pandemic had already shown: in the face of the new and multiple challenges, European cooperation is taking on a new significance.

It is becoming increasingly clear that the EU must provide public assets that the Member States can no longer afford on their own – in the area of security as well as in the area of welfare. The systemic conflict and the increasing division of the world and the global economy into democracies on the one hand and authoritarian regimes on the other are a further strong argument for strengthening the EU as a community so that it better protects the interests of its citizens. In order to do this, however, its decision-making mechanisms must be put to the test: greater democratisation and a new understanding of what it means to be an EU citizen are part of it. Europeans also need to address a key weakness: Unlike China or Russia, for example, the European Union does not have a strong and positive vision of the future for itself, but defines itself in the systemic conflict primarily from a defensive position. But it can and must achieve this in order to cope with the reform tasks that lie ahead: The change is threefold, namely: the green, digital and social transformation which must go hand in hand with a policy that improves internal cohesion, a strengthening of Europe's role in the world – and, to achieve all this, a more appropriately designed governance of the Community.

Global Migration and Cohesion of Diverse Societies

Cornelia Schu

Is there a connection between global migration and the cohesion of diverse societies? What this might look like, and what needs to be done to ensure that they do not become opposites, is the subject of this article. The focus is on the relationship between attitudes in the population; the article deliberately ignores the many other dimensions of the question that have been discussed in various academic disciplines.

Let's start with an observation: the topic of migration played a central role in the French election campaign in 2022 – at least until Russia's invasion of Ukraine. Migration and integration, which is portrayed as a failure, are wonderfully suited as a topic to mobilise people – namely for right-wing populist or right-wing extremist parties that promise to largely stop immigration and, above all, the admission of asylum seekers. Here, the rejection of migration provides cohesion to a certain extent, but only in an in-group and at the price of abandoning the foundations of an open liberal society. In a similar way, immigration has been and continues to be used for mobilisation in other European countries.[1]

Migration and the debate about migration are not the same

For years, the Eurobarometer survey conducted by the European Commission and the European Parliament has repeatedly shown the fundamental concern

---

1 Cf. MIDEM 2019: *Migration and Europe. Annual Report 2019*, Dresden. The report shows that, in the wake of increased numbers of asylum seekers, right-wing populists gained ground in European countries where the issue of migration dominated political discourse.

of many citizens within the European Union regarding migration issues.[2] However, the fact that there is not necessarily a negative correlation between the two issues is demonstrated – to name just one – by the example of Canada, where immigration and multiculturalism have traditionally been part of the self-image. One is therefore well advised to distinguish between empirical migration and the debate about migration. The debate about the transformation of societies through migration should also not allow us to forget that it serves as a focal point for the discomfort with multiple processes of pluralisation and transformation and the resulting signs of fatigue that are observed in modern societies. Examples include the multiplication of ways of life or the diminishing binding effect of institutions such as the church or trade unions, globalisation, and the massive transformations resulting from the fall of the Berlin Wall and the breakup of the former Eastern bloc.

In the following, a few empirical results on the question of social cohesion in Germany and on coexistence in the immigration society will be presented and, on this basis, some suggestions will be derived on how it can be possible to combine migration and cohesion in a liberal democracy.

What does empirical evidence say about cohesion in Germany? One difficulty is that it is notoriously difficult to measure it. There are different approaches to this in research.[3] As an approximation, we will refer here to one of the indicators used, namely membership in society from the perspective of the population. Corresponding questions were asked, for example, in the SVR's (German Expert Council on Migration and Integration) 2016 Integration Barometer, which surveyed the population with and without an immigrant background. Among other things, questions were asked about who actually belongs to German society, which criteria are decisive for this and how people feel they belong here. The results showed that there is a strong sense of belonging to

---

2 The latest survey on the most important global challenges for the future of the EU found that half of Europeans (49%) see climate change at the top, followed by health (34%). Once again, forced migration and displacement are among the top issues (around 30%). When asked about the biggest challenges specifically for the EU, respondents most frequently mention social inequalities (36%), unemployment (32%) and migration issues (31%). In Germany, 37% see this issue as particularly important. Cf. EU Commission/European Parliament (ed.) 2021: *Special Eurobarometer 517: The Future of Europe*, here p. 89 (https://europa.eu/eurobarometer/surveys/detail/2554).

3 Cf. Nicole Deitelhoff, Olaf Groh-Samberg, Matthias Middell (eds.) 2020: *Gesellschaftlicher Zusammenhalt. Ein interdisziplinärer Dialog*, Frankfurt/Main.

society in Germany. The approval ratings were over 90 per cent among respondents without an immigrant background, and about 5 percentage points lower among those with an immigrant background. The least pronounced feelings of belonging were among respondents with a Turkish immigrant background, more than a quarter of whom feel they do not belong to Germany (although almost three quarters feel very much so). Further analyses show a clear connection between the immigrant generation and the intensity of the sense of belonging: respondents from the second generation always feel a stronger sense of belonging than those from the first generation.

Experiences of exclusion were also addressed. The majority of people with a migration background did not feel excluded from society. However, a majority of Muslim persons of Turkish origin felt that people of their origin are excluded from society in Germany.[4] From another study of the SVR research area we know that a visible migration background (e.g. skin colour, headscarf) or an audible migration background (accent) increase the probability that people experience discrimination.[5] That racism and experiences of discrimination have a negative impact on the sense of belonging is generally well established in research.

This raises the question of which criteria determine membership in society in Germany in the eyes of people with and without an immigrant background and what the situation is with regard to the acceptance of migration-related diversity. The SVR discussed this question in its 2021 annual report and evaluated various survey data.[6]

Acceptance of diversity increases

According to the results, the German population's acceptance of diversity has increased, as shown by corresponding long-term data. Immigration is

---

4 Cf. SVR 2016: Viele Götter, ein Staat: Religiöse Vielfalt und Teilhabe im Einwanderungsland. Jahresgutachten 2016 mit Integrationsbarometer, Berlin, and https://www.svr-migration.de/wp-content/uploads/2016/10/Handout_SVR_FB_PK_28_Juni_IB_Zugehoerigkeit.pdf
5 Cf. SVR Research Unit 2018: "Wo kommen Sie eigentlich ursprünglich her?" Experiences of Discrimination and Phenotypical Difference in Germany, Berlin.
6 Cf. for the results summarised briefly below with references to the data sources in detail SVR: Normalfall Diversität? Wie das Einwanderungsland Deutschland mit Vielfalt umgeht. Jahresgutachten, Berlin 2021.

increasingly perceived as enrichment, and immigrants are generally accorded the right to participate. At the same time, the population has come to see immigrants as a part of German society. This is exemplified by the importance respondents attach to certain criteria for granting German citizenship: a majority of respondents consider criteria that can be obtained through one's own efforts, such as a permanent job (and thus independently securing a livelihood), exemption from punishment or a good knowledge of German, to be important for belonging to society. Adapting to the local lifestyle (whatever the respondents understand by this) is also mentioned, and more frequently in 2016 than in 1996 (ALLBUS data). Over time, criteria that the individual cannot influence, such as being born in Germany or having German ancestors, have become significantly less important; membership of a Christian church also plays a comparatively minor role. This tendency is even more pronounced among younger respondents than among older ones.

In addition, the German population is increasingly adopting the principle of equal treatment when it comes to dealing with diversity. One example of this is religious instruction in schools: the proportion of respondents who support the introduction of denominational Muslim religious education has risen steadily over the past 25 years. In 2016, for the first time, it was higher than the proportion of those who would like to see exclusively Christian religious education as a compulsory subject in schools. At the same time, the proportion of those who generally reject religious education as a compulsory subject in state schools is also growing – meaning they are also in favour of equal treatment for all religious communities in Germany.

A robust finding of social science research is that contacts with the other group make a crucial difference to attitudes (the so-called contact hypothesis), and these contacts are increasingly commonplace in societies shaped by immigration – at work, in the neighbourhood and in school and day care.

Germany is increasingly becoming a modern immigration country

What can be concluded from the findings for the research question?

First, the majority of the population in Germany has internalised the transformation into a modern immigration country that has been taking place for a long time. Origin is increasingly seen as less important than the contribution people make here. Principles of equality are gaining in popularity in a diverse society. Unequal treatment is more strongly rejected.

Second, a look at attitudes confirms a conclusion drawn by the SVR in its 2021 annual report: in dealing with increasing diversity, it is important that differences in origin do not become inequalities in participation. This is where politics, state institutions such as schools and the police, but also business and all employers have a role to play. Equal opportunities must be the goal; diversity strategies and the formulation of goals are a means to this end.

Third, newcomers and residents must participate in shaping the community, because co-designing (a liberal conviction) is of central importance, and not only in individual self-interest. As studies by Klaus Böhnke, among others, have shown, social cohesion is also great where people place their faith in self-determination.[7] This active component in a concrete context (be it in the daycare centre or children's school, in a club, in a local district) should not be neglected or underestimated compared to the public meta-debate about cohesion and dealing with diversity. Here, measures that promote and invite engagement make sense.

Fourth, the constant public invocation of social cohesion carries the risk of awakening an expectation of homogeneity or freedom from interference. This can be prevented by self-confidently identifying the acceptance of differences as a component of a pluralistic society. In this society, controversies are part of everyday life and should be conducted as calmly as possible. However, there is still work to be done on this calmness: different views should not be seen or described too quickly as crises. Otherwise, there is a danger of immediately discussing the crisis (of whatever) instead of entering into dialogue with each other about the issues themselves. If, on the other hand, we succeed in conducting this dialogue with composure, self-confidence in our own point of view and empathy for the point of view of others, we can be confident that we will grow socially as a result of negotiation processes. In that case, cohesion would be strengthened without having to explicitly invoke it. Or to put it differently: liberal societies are characterised precisely by the fact that they also establish their cohesion through the civil settlement of their conflicts, a notion that is rejected precisely in illiberal societies in favour of invoking unity and community. In this respect, the factual negotiation of immigration issues in a liberal perspective is not in itself a threat to cohesion. Illiberal, on the other hand, would be the categorical exclusion of plurality and immigration.

---

7   See e.g. Michael Koch, Klaus Boehnke 2016: Kann Bürgerschaftliches Engagement den Zusammenhalt in Deutschland fördern? In: Social Work Theory and Practice 67 (1), pp. 10–20.

Fifth, a key factor in gaining acceptance is the population's perception of integration and migration (policy) and success. Investments in integration policy, in language support and early access to education and the labour market (to name just a few elementary aspects) are therefore central. At the same time, it is important that the state makes use of the options available to it to manage migration.[8] For example, it has been shown that the perception of immigration as too high and unmanaged increases the likelihood that it will be perceived as threatening.[9] In this respect, being a liberal immigration country in which migration and cohesion are positively interrelated means making clear offers and formulating equally clear requirements for newcomers as well as for those already living here for a long time.

---

8   On the limits and possibilities of this control, see SVR 2018: Steuern, was zu steuern ist. SVR Annual Report 2018, Berlin.

9   See, for example, Hannes Weber 2018: Attitudes Towards Minorities in Times of High Migration: A Panel Study among Young Adults in Germany. In: European Sociological Review 2018, pp. 1–19.

Smart Market Design for Sustainable Infrastructures

Achim Wambach

In order to achieve the German government's climate targets, infrastructures play a role that can hardly be overestimated. At the same time, there is hardly any other topic where the conflict between "market or state" is as prevalent as in the expansion of infrastructures. And there are few other areas where focusing on this conflict is so unproductive. What is more relevant is whether the desired results are achieved by monopoly or competition, as well as the question of goal-oriented regulation of monopoly and goal-oriented rules for competition. In economics, these questions fall into the field of "market design".

The design of the competition

The establishment of the "Deregulation Commission" in 1987 by the German government was an expression of a changed view of the desired order of the economy. The commission was tasked with dismantling regulations that were contrary to the market, thereby creating more competition and increasing citizens' freedom of choice. It became apparent that many more stages of the value chain were open to competition than had previously been thought. Why, for example, should one have to rent a telephone set from the post office, while televisions were available on the free market? This orientation of economic policy towards more competition finds its justification in the empirically well-founded economic insight that innovations and the associated welfare benefits are most likely to occur in this market structure.

However, the belief at the time in the competitiveness of some sectors of the economy was overly optimistic. In 1998, for example, the Scientific Working Group for Regulatory Issues at the Regulatory Authority for Telecommunications and Posts stated: "The more successful the regulatory authority's policy is, the more dispensable its regulatory task in the narrower sense becomes. According to all experience, however, a longer period of time must be estimated for the transition from a monopoly-dominated to a competitive market in telecommunications and postal services."[1] Günter Rexrodt, the Federal Minister of Economics at the time, assumed that regulation could give way to general competition supervision after ten years, once competition prevailed. The Federal Network Agency would then be able to abolish itself.[2] Today, however, the Federal Network Agency with its approximately 3,000 employees does not have a guarantee of eternity, but liquidation is certainly not an issue and would not make sense.

The network sectors, and in particular the associated infrastructures, are in fact characterised as "natural monopolies", i.e. monopolies that are compelled by the technical conditions. This is most obvious in the case of the rail network – the construction of a parallel rail network by a competitor would make no sense from an operational or economic point of view. And in the case of such natural monopolies, a regulator is needed to ensure that costs remain under control and that access to the network is not discriminatory. However, this need for a monopoly does not apply to all infrastructures. In the telecommunications sector, for example, infrastructure competition is largely possible; three mobile network operators operate their own networks. However, there are also regions in which network expansion is not economically attractive – the so-called "white spots". Separate regulation is needed to enable expansion there.

We face massive challenges in the 2020s. In the following, I will describe how market design can contribute to the efficient provision of sustainable infrastructures for the sectors that are particularly important for the energy and mobility transition. In the last section, I address the question of whether, with good regulation and good market design, it still matters whether the respective service is provided by market or state.

---

1 Scientific Working Group on Regulatory Issues: *WAR – Leitlinien für Regulierungspolitik*, Bundesnetzagentur, 1998. https://www.bundesnetzagentur.de/SharedDocs/Pressemitt eilungen/DE/1998/980619WAR-Leitlinien.html
2 Taken from Homann, Jochen, *"Geleitwort"* in Bernd Holznagel: *20 Jahre Verantwortung für Netze: Bestandsaufnahme und Perspektiven*, Munich: C.H.Beck 2018.

Energy: Creating markets for security of supply

The energy market is at the heart of the energy transition. For example, the German government plans to convert the power supply from the current 45 per cent to 80 per cent renewable energies by 2030.

The classic field of application of market design is therefore the energy market. The switch to renewable energies will lead to an increase in tenders for wind turbines and solar plants. In these tenders, the amount of compensation is determined. The rules of tendering are a building block of energy market design.

In addition to the switch to renewable energies, there are other tasks: the target triangle of energy policy is an environmentally compatible, affordable and reliable energy supply (§ 1 Energy Industry Act). Security of supply is currently a given in Germany – the local power supply is one of the most secure in the world. In 2020, the average annual power outage lasted just 11 minutes. However, providing this high quality requires repeated regulatory intervention, which will increase when the phase-out of nuclear power and coal is completed and wind and solar power are increasingly used.

From a market design perspective, the question is who can contribute to security of supply at the lowest cost – in other words, how security of supply can also emerge in the market. Many countries, including France and the United Kingdom, use a capacity market to have sufficient and reliable generation capacity available. Scientists are currently discussing whether market-induced supply security can also be ensured by means of mandatory forward contracts. Under these contracts, generators would commit to providing a certain amount of electricity years in advance of the delivery date. By means of such long-term contracts, producers would obtain greater quantity and revenue security and thus also the necessary planning security for adequate investments in a secure supply.

Telecommunications: Vouchers and tenders for "white spots"

Digitisation is an essential building block for the energy transition. One study[3], for example, concludes that the increased use of digital solutions can save around one fifth of today's CO_2 emissions in the next ten years. Increasing digitisation requires a high-performance infrastructure in the telecommunications sector.

Interesting market design issues arise here with regard to the provision of infrastructure, which must be considered separately for the fixed network and the mobile network.

Fixed network

In the fixed network, the copper network (which continues to be regulated), the cable networks and the new fibre-optic networks of different providers are in competition. However, the sluggish expansion of the fibre-optic network has raised the question of whether this market organisation is producing the desired results.

However, this primarily relates to the roll-out of the fibre-optic network in white spots, i.e. in locations where roll-out is not economically viable. It is undisputed that roll-out in these areas, where fibre-optic networks are politically desirable or even part of the general interest, must be supported by government funding. To this end, the federal and state governments have launched a large number of programmes, some of which, however, are leading to over-expansion and crowding out self-supported expansion. In 2019, the Monopolies Commission therefore gave its telecommunications sector report the title "A sense of proportion in network expansion".[4] From a market design perspective, the question also arises as to how a suitable prioritisation of the subsidised expansion can be achieved. One possibility would be to involve the

---

3   Bitkom/Accenture: *Klimaeffekte der Digitalisierung*, Bitkom, 2021. https://www.bitkom.org/Klimaschutz
4   Monopolkommission: *11. Sektorgutachten Telekommunikation (2019): Staatliches Augenmaß beim Netzausbau*, Monopolkommission, 2019. https://www.monopolkommission.de/images/PDF/SG/11sg_telekommunikation.pdf

demand side more in the subsidy in order to obtain an indication of urgency. This can be done via vouchers, which can be used for the switch to fibre optic.[5]

Mobile network

The next allocation of mobile communications frequencies is scheduled to take place in 2023 or 2024, as some of the usage rights currently awarded expire in 2025. The allocation of frequencies essentially determines the future structure of the mobile communications market. For an efficient and competitive market, it is important on the one hand that frequencies are allocated in sufficient quantity and composition to the companies with the most competitive business models. On the other hand, a certain balance must be maintained in the allocation of frequencies among the companies so that competition can develop in the mobile communications market. However, the exact allocation of frequencies to achieve the ideal market structure depends on information that is known exclusively to the individual companies.

In order for the companies' information to be taken into account for allocation, there must be incentives for the companies involved to disclose it. Auction procedures can make this possible and have proven successful in the past for frequency allocation. The advantage of auction procedures is that the companies that derive greater value from the use of the frequencies are generally also more willing to pay and will prevail in a well-designed auction procedure. Auction procedures are also suitable for finding a market structure that benefits downstream competition, for example through allocations for new entrants.

The previous approach of ensuring mobile broadband in the underserved white spots by imposing coverage requirements on all companies successful in the tender is accompanied by problems. In the regions where infrastructure competition functions well, such coverage requirements are irrelevant or even potentially harmful to competition, as they make it more difficult to possibly

---

5   The coalition agreement of the German federal government provides in this regard: "We initiate voucher subsidies where necessary to complement FTTH and in-house fibre cabling." (Bundesregierung: *Mehr Fortschritt wagen: Bündnis für Freiheit, Gerechtigkeit und Nachhaltigkeit*, Bundesregierung, 2021. https://www.bundesregierung.de/resource/blob/974430/1990812/04221173eef9a6720059cc353d759a2b/2021-12-10-koav2021-data.pdf?download=1

differentiate from competitors. In those regions where infrastructure competition is insufficient to ensure a level of coverage deemed necessary, duplication of infrastructure would not be economical. It is therefore more effective to ensure coverage in these areas by only one of the network operators and to give the other operators access, for example through roaming.

To this end, a separate "white spot auction" could be held, i.e. a reverse (negative) subsidy auction for expansion in these regions. An illustrative example of this is provided by Denmark, which went down this route in 2012 as part of the LTE spectrum auction. The special feature was that for three particularly sparsely populated regions, each bidder had an expansion obligation, but the bidders could bid in the auction for an exception to this basic expansion obligation. In other words, a bidder could submit four bids at the same time, with expansion obligations in none, one, two or all three regions. At the end of the auction, the winning bid combination was the one that generated the highest revenue, taking into account that at least one of the bidders assumed the expansion obligation in each of the three regions.[6]

Rail: Using the Deutschlandtakt to boost competition

A central task for the mobility revolution will be the development of a modern, low-emission mobility system. However, the German rail system is already problematic today: it appears to be downright "inherited"; in long-distance transport, for example, Deutsche Bahn has a market share of a good 95 per cent in terms of transport capacity. Quality problems are the result.[7]

The fact that the rail network is owned by Deutsche Bahn AG has undoubtedly also contributed to this, and this repeatedly gives rise to opportunities for discrimination in favour of the train service operators of its own group. There

---

6   The coalition agreement stipulates that "frequency allocation should be geared towards specifications for area coverage, and negative auctions should also be used." (Federal Government (2021): *Mehr Fortschritt wagen: Bündnis für Freiheit, Gerechtigkeit und Nachhaltigkeit*, Bundesregierung. https://www.bundesregierung.de/resource/blo b/974430/1990812/04221173eef9a6720059cc353d759a2b/2021-12-10-koav2021-data.p df?download=1
7   See in this regard: Monopolkommission: 7. *Sektorgutachten Bahn (2019): Mehr Qualität und Wettbewerb auf die Schiene, Monopolkommission*, 2019. https://www.monopolkomm ission.de/images/PDF/SG/7sg_bahn_volltext.pdf

are no limits to the imagination: how are construction sites handled? What are the rules when tracks are full at stations? How high are the charges for rail use?

The planned Deutschlandtakt (German Pace) offers a new opportunity for more competition. The aim is to coordinate train connections throughout Germany at half-hourly or hourly intervals and to reduce travel times. This will mean that there will then be clearly defined train path "slots" which, in principle, allow a separate allocation rule, i.e. the allocation of individual routes at certain times to competitors as well. The Monopolies Commission recommends such a tender or concession model.[8] The competitive dynamics that tenders have brought about in regional transport – where Deutsche Bahn AG's competitors now have a market share of almost 30 per cent – could thus also be transferred to long-distance transport.

Market or state: An outdated dichotomy

As has become clear up to this point, the first question to be asked when building infrastructures is to what extent the respective goal can be achieved through competitive structures or to what extent recourse must be taken to a company which then holds the infrastructure monopoly in each case. Consistent regulation of the monopolist and targeted rules for the market will then ensure efficient construction and operation of the infrastructure.

The question of state ownership of companies is thus no longer in the foreground, but it does not become irrelevant either. State ownership always becomes problematic when there are conflicts of interest on the part of the public sector, since in such cases it acts both as a rule-maker and as an actor.

This became clear, for example, with the amendment of the Postal Act, which has been largely unchanged since 1997. Since May 2020, the Federal Ministry of Economics and Technology has had a draft for a "major" amendment to the Postal Act that would have strengthened competition on the postal markets. However, only a "minor" amendment to the Postal Act came out in the last legislative period until autumn 2021. The Chairman of the Monop-

---

8 Monopolkommission: *8. Sektorgutachten Bahn (2021): Wettbewerb in den Takt!*, Monopolkommission, 2021. https://www.monopolkommission.de/images/PDF/SG/8 sg_bahn_volltext.pdf

olies Commission, Prof. Jürgen Kühling, commented: "The 'small' Postal Act amendment was inadequate ... and also favoured Deutsche Post AG."[9]

On the occasion of the handover of office at the Federal Ministry of Economics and Climate Protection in December 2021, Minister Dr Robert Habeck said: "We need ... a pragmatic approach. Ideological debate [should] not become the signature of the next four years, but success. Debates about whether there should be more or less government, whether there should be more regulation or deregulation, [are] actually ... misplaced."[10] In recent decades, economics has contributed to the de-ideologisation of the debate under the buzzword of market design. What is tested, deployed and then evaluated is what ultimately works. These methodologies and findings should be increasingly applied in German politics in the expansion and use of sustainable infrastructures.

---

9   Monopolkommission Pressemitteilung: Die Monopolkommission stellt ihr 12. Sektorgutachten zum Wettbewerb auf den Postmärkten vor „Wettbewerb mit neuem Schwung!", Monopolkommission, 2021. https://www.monopolkommission.de/images/PDF/SG/presse_12sg_post.pdf

10 Habeck, Robert: Amtsübergabe im Wirtschaftsministerium: Rede Dr. Robert Habeck, Bundesministerium für Wirtschaft und Klimaschutz, [online] https://www.bmwi.de/Redaktion/DE/Downloads/P-R/08122021-rede-habeck-amtsübergabe.pdf?__blob=publicationFile&v=10 [retrieved 25.01.2022].

The Future of Free Trade

Gabriel Felbermayr

Free trade is once again out of fashion, and with countries like Russia it is currently completely unthinkable. But even in peacetime, proponents of open markets have never had it easy in history, as Douglas Irwin brilliantly describes in his classic *Free Trade under Fire*, now in its fifth edition.[1]

Free trade under fire

Nonetheless, there seems to be a rhythm to the debate. Opponents of free trade build arguments as to why tariffs and other barriers are necessary. Their thought patterns often seem plausible at first glance. They find political support. Proponents of free trade usually need some time to expose the logical fallacies of the protectionists. They are often helped by empiricism, because erecting barriers does not usually solve a problem. Then, after some time of open-market policies, new justifications for protectionism emerge. In the past, for example, it was often a matter of protecting an established social order, preserving good and secure jobs, or promoting a more equal distribution of income. Today, the old argument that free trade endangers national sovereignty is being brought up again. And with unprecedented intensity, a trade-off is being made between sustainability and free trade. In the acute phase of the coronavirus crisis, it was even suggested that globalisation endangered health. And so free trade is currently in a trough of popularity.

The coalition agreement of the German government reflects this mood. The term free trade appears once in the text, apart from a heading, and there only under limitations. It is to exist only on the basis of fair social, environmental

---

1   Irwin, Douglas: Free Trade under Fire. Princeton: Princeton University Press 2020.

and human rights standards.[2] In the new trade policy doctrine of the European Union, free trade is not a goal per se. Establishing and preserving open markets is just one task of trade policy, along with sustainability and strategic autonomy. And even in the U.S., after the explicit protectionism of Donald Trump, there is no enthusiasm for free trade under the leadership of Joe Biden.

Yet the Covid crisis in particular highlighted the benefits of open markets very clearly. It is true that in Germany, too, the assembly lines came to a standstill when, at the beginning of the pandemic, Chinese and later northern Italian factories went into lockdown. Imported primary products were suddenly missing. Then it was discovered in Europe that certain medical products such as masks and reagents or packaging materials were not available in the required quantities on the world markets. Globalisation sceptics of all stripes were quick to point out the lack of reliability of global supply chains and called for new regulation and subsidies to bring production back to Europe.

But this argument quickly collapsed. If global trade had plunged 15 per cent from pre-crisis levels in April 2020, it bounced back just as quickly, exceeding those levels again four months later.[3] By November 2021, global trade was almost eight per cent above pre-crisis levels (December 2019). Global industrial production fared quite similarly, quickly climbing back above pre-crisis levels.

The advantage of open markets is also evident during the covid pandemic

A perfect V formation occurred, foreseen by few, and, after overcoming the initial Covid shock, a veritable boom in global trade. The globalised economy satisfied the increased demand for many goods: protective clothing and consumer durables from China, machinery from Europe, raw materials from all over the world. Even more, it enabled the rapid scaling of global vaccine production. In 2021, starting from scratch, more than 9 billion vaccine doses were produced and distributed, taking advantage of global value networks. The globalised economy has delivered – contrary to all prophecies of doom.

---

2   Coalition Agreement 2021 – 2025 between the Social Democratic Party of Germany (SPD), Alliance 90/The Greens and the Free Democrats (FDP): Dare more progress. Alliance for Freedom, Justice and Sustainability.
3   WTO: »Trade Statistics and Outlook. Global trade rebound beats expectations but marked by regional divergences«, Press Release WTO, 4.10.2021.

However, Germany currently seems to be disconnected from this dynamic. This is in stark contrast to the past, where strong growth in world trade has always led to a boom in German industry. This is not getting off the ground in Germany, and hasn't since mid-2017. The country may be suffering more than others from supply bottlenecks and material shortages. However, the significantly better industrial activity in countries with similar specialisation profiles shows that the stagnating production in the manufacturing sector probably has more to do with a weakness in Germany as a business location than with a lull in global trade.

It is interesting to compare the Covid crisis with the last recession, the global economic and financial crisis of 2008/09. At that time, too, there was a rapid and severe slump in world trade and global industrial production. But the recovery took much longer. It was not until 24 months after the collapse of the Lehman Brothers investment bank that the two variables reached pre-crisis levels. The reason is that at that time it was a financial market crisis that required a painful clean-up of banks' and companies' balance sheets. The Covid crisis, on the other hand, is interruptive by its very nature: functioning production structures are repeatedly interrupted by regulatory requirements, but in many cases can be quickly restarted. And because governments and central banks all over the world provided liquidity in a historically unique way, there were no corporate bankruptcies during the shutdown phases. Many market participants had expected a repeat of the long recession that followed the Lehman bankruptcy and reduced their capacities as a precaution – a miscalculation that can be seen as one cause of the current tight supply.

However, the global boom had led to an explosion in prices. This is a logical consequence when demand expands surprisingly strongly, but the supply side is repeatedly interrupted by new Covid measures. The average price of industrial raw materials temporarily rose by almost 70% above the pre-crisis level and is still 45% higher in the latest data; fossil fuels are 70% more expensive. The Ukraine war and the EU's move away from fossil fuel imports from Russia are reinforcing this trend. Freight rates in international goods transportation have also exploded, increasing more than fivefold on some routes. As a result, producer prices have risen sharply. In Germany, they are 24 per cent higher in November 2021 than in the same month a year earlier. There have not been such increases since the early 1950s. Supply problems and high prices have therefore stifled the boom. However, they have not triggered a downturn, and there is considerable upside potential.

This is because high prices invite production expansions. More cargo ships were ordered in 2021 than at any time in the last two decades. Commodity cartels like OPEC try to keep prices high through shortages, but that rarely succeeds, and certainly not in the long run. Even if the war in Ukraine initially leads to new records in commodity prices, there is much to suggest that in the long term the shortages on the world markets will ease and prices will fall – in the medium term at all events. In the short term, however, geostrategic tensions threaten further trouble. Russia and Ukraine, although of minor importance in macroeconomic terms, are world powers in natural gas, oil, grains and some metals. If their supply is withheld from the global economy, there will be a lasting threat of energy shortages and hunger in countries of the Global South. This could remain a major issue for a long time. One consequence of climate change will be greater volatility in food prices, with periods of high rates of price increase.

Covid does not challenge the global economy based on division of labour

Nevertheless, the coronavirus crisis does not challenge the global economic model based on the division of labour; rather, the opposite is true. Global trade has made it possible to quickly overcome the worst economic dislocations in the first place. Simulation studies show that decoupling supply chains reduces international contagion effects from global trade – you immunise yourself against production failures abroad – but the costs in terms of lost growth outweigh the benefits many times over.

The international division of labour is also extremely helpful in overcoming other global challenges. This is because, globally speaking, it has a productivity-enhancing effect: each country's scarce resources are systematically deployed in those sectors where the country has its comparative advantages. In those sectors where the resources would be used relatively unproductively, they are imported. If we want to cope well with the climate crisis, the world will have to become much more productive with energy very quickly – the international division of labour will help here. And the growing scarcity of labour – not only in Europe, but also in Asia – makes it more necessary to find ways to use it more productively. Here, too, the international division of labour helps. And it does so without the need for large government-orchestrated investment programmes or expensive subsidies.

Unfortunately, there is a lot wrong with the international trade in goods. As mentioned, the current supply problems are the result of misjudgements by managers who assumed a slow, at best U-shaped recovery. The probability of supply shortfalls was also underestimated. This made it seem rational to keep inventories as tight as possible and the number of suppliers low. These mistakes are costing many companies sales and profits: despite high demand, some orders cannot be filled. Companies are therefore diversifying their supplier networks and changing their inventory strategies. In accordance with the logic of the market economy, they have strong incentives to do this; they do not need any government requirements to do so. However, the state should ensure that the diversification of networks is supported by modern free trade agreements and that solutions are found to the shortage of building sites for warehouses. In both respects, not much is currently happening in Europe and Germany.

The state should support through free trade agreements

Much more problematic, however, is the strain on global trade in goods caused by increasing political risks. The trade war between the U.S. and China is far from over, and with it the risk that products from European manufacturers in China will suddenly be burdened by high tariffs in the U.S., and vice versa. In addition, there could also be additional tariffs for products finished in Europe if preliminary products from China or the USA are used in their manufacture. The new rules in the trade agreement between the U.S., Mexico and Canada, which restrict inputs from outside the zone, show how this could work.

But European trade policy is also becoming more protectionist. The proposed supply chain law requires additional, expensive bureaucracy to monitor foreign suppliers and exposes companies to the risk of heavy penalties if they fail to meet their due diligence obligations to the letter of the law. The use of trade policy instruments to pursue foreign policy objectives in the areas of human rights, social or environmental policy creates new barriers. One example is carbon offsets, which will create new risks and costs in international trade. And even if no concrete action is taken at all, increasing uncertainty and tensions with trading partners from Russia to the United Kingdom are weighing on business.

Companies are confronting these risks. In concrete terms, this very often means bringing production closer to end customers to reduce political risks.

For the Chinese market, production takes place in China; for the American market, production takes place in the USA, Mexico or Canada, including upstream products. For a relatively small, open economy like Germany's, which has benefited more than any other from overseas exports, this is not good news. Nor is it good news for consumers, because forgoing the benefits of the international division of labour means higher prices. Of course, all this does not mean that internationally positioned German companies cannot be successful in a world of greater trade barriers. It's just that value creation is increasingly taking place abroad, not in Germany.

But one thing is probably inevitable: the overdue decarbonisation of international transportation will dampen the trade in goods. If the ocean giants have to pay adequate prices for their CO_2 emissions, the author estimates that global trade in goods will decline by 10 to 15 per cent. In contrast to harmful protectionism, however, this would be a welcome development, because trade can only create sustainable prosperity if costs are kept true. If transportation becomes more expensive, this strengthens small-scale trade, including cross-border trade, of course. However, politically enforced regionalism or economic nationalism will certainly not contribute to the success of the energy transition. Green energy must in any case be internationally tradable and produced where the comparative advantages for it exist.

But trade in goods is not the whole story. While everyone, including the author of these lines, is looking at trade in goods, trade in services is developing more dynamically. There, the internet plays a large and growing role. New technologies such as blockchain and artificial intelligence are making cross-border business possible in a way that did not exist before. There is a new wave building here that can change globalisation – away from physical goods to virtually traded services, to medical and legal services, to finance, entertainment and much more.

So we are not dealing with the end of globalisation, but with its transformation. Policymakers should allow this transformation to take place and shape it in a spirit of international cooperation rather than protectionist compartmentalisation.

I Tweet, therefore I am? For a New Ethics of Digitalisation

Alexandra Borchardt

They were among the saddest scenes this pandemic had to offer: nurses holding tablet computers in front of the faces of terminally ill Covid patients to at least give them the illusion that their loved ones were close to them. Even though the term Zoom fatigue claims its place in the German vernacular, none of this would have happened without digitisation: the ability to break through loneliness, create feelings of connectedness, stay connected and convey messages, even in the most challenging situations. Those who like it less emotional can think of more mundane benefits, such as the fact that many employees have been able to earn a living and be cared for even under conditions of isolation thanks to the networked world. All of this can be called freedom. Without digital communication channels, this pandemic would have been a different story.

However, the situation is not clear-cut. For every argument that celebrates the possibilities of digitisation, there is another that invokes its dangers. Yes, we have new, individual freedoms. Many of us can now work wherever we want, communicate without limits, compare offers and store across the web. Thanks to the platform economy, a world market can theoretically be tapped from all corners of the globe. People can rent server capacity in data clouds, do their banking before they even get out of bed, and educate themselves at low cost. Compared to everything that capitalism had demanded of the inhabitants of the purely analogue world, digital structures have empowered consumers and entrepreneurs. And civil liberties have grown as well. We can all use a wide variety of channels to inform ourselves, express ourselves, represent ourselves, intervene politically and, if necessary, seek allies around the globe. The importance of the printing press is dwindling; everyone can be their own publisher.

Digitisation changes the world as we know it

But digitisation is also ending freedom as we know it. When everything is networked, hardly anyone can act undetected. Our paths, our habits, our preferences, our spending, our performance – more and more of what used to remain without trace or disappear into isolated files now feeds mountains of data that we don't know will eventually become graveyards or be used against us. Where algorithms ceaselessly sort data points, turn bestsellers into top sellers and push less-sought-after items into the stockpile of oblivion, we sometimes wonder what we still decide for ourselves and where, in reality, decisions are made for us. Applications or credit requests are sorted out by software before a human being has sifted through them. The individual and his or her potential disappear in extrapolations. Anyone who reads Dave Eggers' novel *The Every*, a bitter dystopia about an all-controlling corporation, will find it hard to laugh.[1] In the real world, the analogue book, which you can read without being tracked, still holds its own. Cash, on the other hand, once the key to freedom, has already been phased out in some places. There is every reason to be concerned about freedom in the digitalised world.

It's debatable who poses the greatest threat to this freedom. Is it the tech companies of Silicon Valley, whose business models in the social networks reward the loud and crass and thus make cultivated debates so difficult? Many feel degraded from citizen to consumer, made so drowsy by the convenience of digitally available services that they don't even feel how they are being led on the leash of algorithms. Critical literature on the tech giants has become a genre in its own right, with even former bigwigs in the business knitting away at this narrative.

In countries where despots and autocrats rule, the verdict on Facebook (recently Meta) and Google is milder. Where surveillance, control and propaganda are part of everyday life and people are struggling bit by bit for information and freedom of opinion, many people seize every opportunity to network. The digital world enables them to live more openly, ideally in solidarity. They accept the side effects, even if many know: every step they take on the net makes them more transparent, more controllable, more vulnerable. The internet offers both the possibility of subversive information and action and the possibility of comprehensive control, even digital totalitarianism. China is a pioneer on this path, and others are following.

---

1   Eggers, Dave: The Every. New York: Hamish Hamilton 2021.

Shaping digitisation

But there is another way. There has to be a different way. We have to shape the digital world instead of letting ourselves be shaped. We need to catch up. The early prophets of digitisation may have called for freedom, but they didn't think it through to the end. The "wisdom of the many" quickly became the tyranny of the loud. Freedom without rules gives the right to the strongest; it leads to anarchy or dictatorship. Hatred and agitation on the internet muzzle instead of empower. In a democracy, the right belongs to freedom like the door belongs to the home. Freedom of expression is elementary, but without separation of powers and the rule of law, the individual is left unprotected. It is true that the law also applies in the digitalised world, but it is just too slow. What is needed is a new ethic of digitisation that applies to everyone: governments, companies and every individual citizen. Freedom, law and responsibility – only as a triumvirate do they serve people.

It gives us hope that politics and society will no longer leave it up to the tech companies to decide what works and what doesn't in the digital space. Technology is just a tool. It can intensify social problems, but it can also contribute to their solutions. The responsibility for this does not lie with the internet companies alone. The Ethics of Digitalisation project, for example, has explored how technological progress can be underpinned by values.[2] Under the patronage of German President Frank-Walter Steinmeier, internet research institutes around the globe were involved in the project. Over a period of two years, 151 scientists from 51 countries around the world racked their brains over central questions: how can debates on social networks be moderated in such a way that freedom of expression is preserved, and hate is minimised? How must algorithms be developed so that they do not discriminate? What could a networked city look like that serves people and does not degrade them to the appendage of a tech utopia? How can and must digital education be structured so that everyone benefits? The diversity of topics that this project has only been able to touch on alone shows how broad and deep the debate needs to be. And the global approach makes it clear that it must be freed from the ping-pong between Europe and the USA with China as the laughing third on the sidelines.

---

2 »Ethik der Digitalisierung – von Prinzipien zu Praktiken«, Alexander von Humboldt Institut für Internet und Gesellschaft. https://www.hiig.de/project/ethik-der-digitalisierung/

Countries in Africa and Southeast Asia have different things to gain and lose from digitisation than those in the Western world.

But what should the ethics of digitisation in a liberal world look like? There is no blueprint for this, but a few principles should apply. Here are seven ideas that could be a start.

First, individual freedom and self-determination must be safeguarded. A liberal society relies on the power of individuals and their interaction in a fair, pluralistic competition. Diversity is the key to social and economic innovation and prosperity. In a world of digital ratings, likes and clicks, where rankings and projections always promote the bestseller and automatically screen out the less popular, individuality is left behind. Humans also discriminate and intimidate, but software tends to potentiate stereotypes and errors. Artificial intelligence often sets the course for life. Algorithms must therefore be regularly checked to ensure they are free of discrimination. People need ways of obtaining justice quickly and easily in cases of doubt. There's no question that a wealth of data can provide beneficial insights. But be careful, calculations are not facts. Even in a digital society, individual cases must be taken into account.

Second, we need communication platforms that promote quality and build trust. Billions of people are on social networks and search engines these days, but only about one in four say they trust them.[3] No wonder, because there it is difficult to distinguish between what is serious content and what has been flushed down the timeline because of other characteristics, especially because it is somehow shrill or voyeuristic. The platform companies' business models, which rely on ad revenue, make sure of that, because they target the mass of views and interactions. It is naive to believe that users can be redirected from one platform to another, "better" platform just like that – after all, most use a particular site because their acquaintances, colleagues, friends or loved ones do too, or because they, like media brands, want to reach certain users. So ground rules must apply within platforms.

One of the smartest ideas is that, instead of focusing on moderating and deleting objectionable or illegal content, more and more posts should be labelled with quality seals that come from trustworthy institutions and thus be upgraded in the automatic sorting process. This is the core of the Journalism Trust Initiative, initiated by Reporters Without Borders with the support of

---

3   Reuters Institute for the Study of Journalism: Digital News Report. https://www.digitalnewsreport.org

the European Broadcasting Union and the AFP news agency.[4] Organisations that want such a seal must be certified, modelled on the industry's self-regulation through DIN standards. Making problematic posts less visible in this way, rather than deleting them, strengthens quality and freedom of expression in equal measure. The biggest political issue is the question: what has to go off the net? Some demand that social networks should delete "harmful content". Those who suffer under repressive governments fear from painful experience that this would be a gateway for censorship. The only thing everyone agrees on is what the Council of Europe also recommends: consistently and swiftly remove what violates the law.[5] Even in the digital age, freedom of expression remains a fundamental right and a pillar of democracy.[6]

Third, technological logic must not crush humanity and creativity with efficiency. The logic of technology is that of optimisation. Artificial intelligence calculates solutions from data – the more of it there is, the more accurate the recommendation. We know this from digital route planners: everything is heading towards an apparently optimal solution. What lies to the right and left of the path is ignored. The goal is the greatest possible efficiency. But as strange as it may sound, efficiency is the enemy of innovation. Innovation requires a willingness to experiment, the ability to link things that at first glance don't belong together, to solve problems radically differently than existing technologies suggest. If Apple had only optimised the mobile phone, the iPhone would not exist. If you only ever make coal-fired power plants cleaner, you won't achieve an energy revolution. Many great inventions were based on surprising observations. In their book *The Imagination Machine*, Martin Reeves and Jack Fuller describe how organisations can free themselves from the corset of efficiency and systematically train imagination.[7] A free society thrives on thinking that breaks boundaries. Life is predictable to a limited extent.

---

4 See Journalism Trust Initiative. https://www.journalismtrustinitiative.org/
5 Committee of experts on freedom of expression and digital technologies: »Draft Recommendation of the Committee of Ministers to member States on the impacts of digital technologies on freedom of expression«, Council of Europe, 21.9.2021. https://rm.coe.int/msi-dig-2020-05-draft-recommendation-on-the-impact-of-digital-technolo/1680a43c8e
6 The author was an expert and rapporteur in the Council of Europe's Committee of Experts on »Freedom of Expression and Digital Technologies« in the period 2020/2021 and therefore contributed to the corresponding recommendation.
7 Reeves, Martin & Fuller, Jack: The Imagination Machine. How to Spark Ideas and Create Your Company's Future, Watertown: Harvard Business Review Press 2021.

Fourth, societal problems must be solved by society, not by technology. Technology is seductive. Who doesn't wish that obstacles could be removed at the push of a button, that all diseases could be cured with a tablet – and with as few side effects as possible? Technology can be a blessing, but it tempts us to rely too heavily on it. Many a company believes that with the right technology, digitisation is a made bed. That digital change is above all cultural change, affecting the power relations between senders and receivers, is something many first have to painfully learn. A shiny, beautiful technological world can conceal a lot, but you shouldn't rely on it. Automated deletion in social networks demonstrates the limits of technology when it comes to nuances, cultural diversity and different sensitivities. Without people, nothing works. Sometimes technology reveals where the problems lie. American society was polarised long before social networks existed. But the ability for groups to now band together more quickly and effectively has supersized the conflicts. With some courage, one might say that is good, because only where fractures are visible can repair begin.

Fifth, liberal society needs civic engagement. Political participation in the digital society, that looks like a convenient thing to do. A petition is quickly liked, a comment posted. I tweet, therefore I am? That's a make-believe world. Civic engagement and political participation are exhausting. They demand commitment, work, effort and attention to detail. In Silicon Valley, there are those who believe politics has had its day. A kind of digitally controlled super-administration is all that citizens need. This fails to recognise that politics is the art of negotiating between different views and interests. Democracy thrives in the struggle to find the solution that best mediates between divergent interests.

Sixth, at the heart of a free society is education – digital education for all. Education is a promise of advancement; it is the key to transcending social classes. Opportunities for education have never been as high as in the digital world, where there are an infinite number of offerings free of charge via the internet. And yet they are rarely used by those who could benefit from them the most. The goal must be to whet the appetites for lifelong education of people from all walks of life. The formats for this are more diverse than ever – from linear reading to podcast listening to gaming and virtual reality, everyone should be able to find something that meets their learning needs. Generations can learn from each other; what an opportunity! Digital education is part of basic education. How do you research on the internet, how do you behave there, how do you check information, what can you do and what should you not do?

These must become cultural techniques for everyone. If we want to shape the digital world, we have to understand it.

Seventh, independent media needs protection and strengthening. Journalism is often called the fourth estate; in any case, it is a pillar of democracy. Where people have access to independent media, they go to the polls more often, run for political office more often, and municipal finances are better managed because an outside authority is watching over the actors. Public broadcasting – and not state broadcasting disguised as such – stabilises democracy.[8] The time of the gatekeepers is over, some argue; thanks to social networks, people can manage the big debate without help. The flood of allegations and lies that is sweeping through the internet demonstrates the opposite. People need reliable information to orient themselves, to form an opinion, to make a decision. The pandemic has shown that, in case of doubt, this can save lives.

---

8   European Broadcasting Union: »News Report: What's Next? Public Service Journalism in the Age of Distraction, Opinion and Information Abundance«, 22.11.2021. https://www.ebu.ch/publications/strategic/loginonly/report/news-report---whats-next-public-service-journalism-in-the-age-of-distraction-opinion-and-information-abundance

Liberty Politics as Democracy Politics

Christopher Gohl

In 2022, liberal democracies find themselves in a fourfold stress test: polarised from within, threatened by enemies of the system from without, challenged by megatrends such as climate and demographic change. The fourth front is homemade: the failure to bid farewell to unfruitful orthodoxies and to establish contemporary forms of liberal coexistence.

However, this is probably also where the path to re-energising liberal democracies begins. To do so, we should remember the great strength of liberal systems – their ability to learn. Since Kant at the latest, the mother of all emancipation, it begins with self-criticism. At the same time, it is part of the source code of an ever vigilant freedom policy, with which we maintain and further develop liberal search and learning systems. Freedom policy is first and foremost democracy policy, and it must become a strength in the stress test – with the model of a learning democracy.

Self-criticism opens up new paths

Self-criticism, Timothy Garton Ash reminds us, has been a liberal strength ever since Arnold Ruge's "Self-Criticism of Liberalism" of 1843.[1] Ash himself faults liberalism's self-distortion to a one-dimensional apology of free markets and private capital. He rightly observes that liberalism has left concerns about community and identity to conservatives and concerns about equality and solidarity to socialists, rather than providing answers from the rich tapestry of lib-

---

1   Ash, Timothy G.: »The Future of Liberalism«, in Prospect Magazine December 9, 2020. https://www.prospectmagazine.co.uk/magazine/the-future-of-liberalism-brex it-trump-philosophy

eral traditions. He blames this on a plutocratically appropriated elite of liberal Davos-goers, nominally the Clintons and Tony Blair.

They must also accept criticism from Michael Sandel. In his *Tyranny of Merit* he also mentions Barack Obama and Gerhard Schröder.[2] They would all have represented the puritanical motif of the meritocracy of the market, newly popularised by Ronald Reagan, according to which the poor underclass had not forged their own fortunes well enough (for example, had not absorbed enough education); for which they themselves bore the moral blame. It takes little imagination to relate Sandel's critique to Guido Westerwelle's phrase about the "late Roman decadence" of Germany's Hartz IV benefit of 2010. For Sandel, this shows the "tyranny of meritocracy": elites who have become arrogant and competent despise the broad masses (Hillary Clinton's "basket of deplorables"), which then triggers illiberal populism. Sandel counters this with the idea of respect, with which he inspired the SPD's 2021 election campaign.

Even if one thinks this criticism is exaggerated, it can sensitise. After all, the distinctions of *globalists* versus *localists* and *virtuals* versus *practicals* or the narratives of the libertarian conservative *Free America* and the meritechnocratic *Smart America* (both liberty-minded) distinguished by George Packer sound similar. Both are criticised by the white, Christian and nationalist *Real America* and the woke *Just America*.[3] Packer hopes for the *Equal America* of a fair shake that he prompts Joe Biden[4] – which in turn comes close to Sandel's hope that Biden, like Olaf Scholz before him, might after all embrace the motif of respect endowed by Sandel.[5]

Perhaps the social obliviousness of liberal elites criticised here is due to the dreamlike coma of the liberal victory of 1989 (according to Amichai Magen in this volume). For even though the idea of sustainable development within planetary boundaries reached the general public for the first time with the 1992

---

2 Sandel, Michael J.: The Tyranny of Merit: What's Become of the Common Good? London: Penguin Books 2020.
3 Packer, George: »How America Fractured into Four Parts«, in: The Atlantic, July/August 2021 issue. https://www.theatlantic.com/magazine/archive/2021/07/george-packer-four-americas/619012/
4 Packer, George: The Fifth Narrative, in: The Atlantic, August 15, 2021. https://www.theatlantic.com/ideas/archive/2021/08/bidens-agenda-is-equal-america/619751/
5 Wallace-Wells, Benjamin: »A Political Philosopher Is Hopeful About the Democrats«, in: The New Yorker December 12, 2021. https://www.newyorker.com/news/annals-of-inquiry/a-political-philosopher-is-hopeful-about-the-democrats.

Earth Summit in Rio de Janeiro, nothing seemed to stand in the way of freedom's triumphant march in the form of a "free trade zone from Vancouver to Vladivostok". Liberal constitutions, treaties and regulatory dismantling would first bring painful structural change, but then prosperity over a world of industrious and educated people.

The disappointed expectations of a global triumph of freedom prompted the Tübingen philosopher of freedom Claus Dierksmeier as early as 2016 to identify a central defect in the source code of liberal theory and practice: a reductionist dumbed-down idea of "quantitative freedom" that is wholly uninterested in contexts and purposes and outrageously imperial in effect.[6] Dierksmeier traces slogans such as "more freedom, less state" and the neoliberal deregulation programmes of the Washington Consensus to an economistic stripping of freedom, according to which freedom grows up proportionally to the abolition of moral urge, moral inclination and legal compulsion: "The more freedom, the better."

As a consequence, liberal contract theories or rational choice thinking, but also liberal parties, might understand claims to solidarity, ecological responsibility, common good, generational justice, security or even justice of opportunity and even everyday consideration only as a quantitative minus of freedom, not as its expression. Freedom becomes the largest possible bubble of independence, which is supposed to end where the independence of the next person begins – a static notion that prevents the intelligent shaping of conditions of freedom in a liberal, open, diverse and, precisely for that reason, interdependent world.

Freedom policy between paralysis and emancipation

By recommending that freedom be understood not first as a quantitative stop sign, but as a qualitative signpost ("the better, the more"), Dierksmeier also wants to overcome the paralysing poison of the distinction between negative and positive freedom. Freedoms, he points out, always have a negative and a positive dimension: only positively distinguished forms of freedom can also be negatively protected from their restriction. The categorically nonsensical opposition of both forms of freedom turns out to be a shot in the knee of liberal politics.

---

6   Dierksmeier, Claus: Qualitative Freiheit. Bielefeld: transcript 2016.

It is true that the opposition of negative and positive freedom is practically popular. Negative liberty corresponds to the moral intuition of finding heteronomy bad.[7] It lends itself to quick liberal reflexes. But the (often conservative) friends of negative freedom are all too happy to use it to insist only on protecting the status quo or maximising their own freedom without acknowledging the freedom claims of others. The (often progressive) friends of positive freedom, on the other hand – themselves morally motivated by motives of fairness and caring – are happy to restrict the freedoms of others in the name of the freedoms they particularly love.

This clash of freedoms follows the quantitative logic of the zero-sum game. The disjunction of negative and positive liberty paralyses its adherents because it fails to identify the means and conditions of constructive libertarian conflict management. Instead of understanding, as Ash and Möllers[8] do, the historical diversity of the liberal "tradition of traditions"[9] as a constitutive and powerful source of liberal progress, liberal history of ideas remains only the chronicle of an irreconcilable war of positions over the consistent (negative or positive) interpretation of a truly "classical liberalism".

Dierksmeier is different. He substantiates the necessity and conditions of an everyday politics of freedom that knows how to weigh, dignify, order, organise, regulate, protect, strengthen, criticise and correct various claims to freedom and the fulfilment of freedom. "Self-determination in cosmopolitan responsibility", as the subtitle of his book reads, requires open-ended search and learning processes in which freedom becomes the mode and measure of its self-correction. Dierksmeier, following Karl Christian Friedrich Krause, John Dewey and Amartya Sen, calls this "freedom as a method": freedom ends are to be determined with freedom means, the idea of freedom is to be brought again and again to terms that correspond to the circumstances of contemporary history. Not by philosophy, but, Dierksmeier agrees with Sen's life chances approach, civically and politically by the people concerned themselves.[10]

---

7 Haidt, Jonathan: The Righteous Mind: Why Good People are Divided by Politics and Religion, London: Penguin Books 2012.
8 Möllers, Christoph: Freiheitsgrade.Elemente einer liberalen politischen Mechanik. Berlin: Suhrkamp 2020.
9 Shklar, Judith N./Bajohr, Hannes (Hg.): Der Liberalismus der Rechte, Berlin: Matthes & Seitz 2017.
10 Sen, Amartya: Development as Freedom. Oxford: University Press 1999.

Thus, everyday freedom politics in the spirit of "qualitative freedom" creates the conditions of constant self-liberation. It ensures what Christoph Möllers calls "a practice of openness to results" that "enables processes of which it must be unclear where they lead".[11] To justify this, Dierksmeier reconstructs the liberal tradition itself as a civilisational process of searching and learning, the object of which are ideas and concepts of freedom that permanently prove themselves in liberal coexistence. This corresponds to Stefan Kolev's "adaptive liberalism"[12] and makes concrete what Amichai Magen describes rather abstractly with the selection of valid orders of freedom by "cold evolutionary logic".

Freedom policy means first of all (1) regulatory policy as concern for the basic order of fair and humanising institutions and procedures, rules and rights. At the same time, it encompasses (2) opportunity policy with the goal of guaranteeing life chances for everyone, as well as (3) the cultivation of lifestyles of responsible freedom. Inspired by Dierksmeier, Germany's Free Democratic Party (FDP), for example, took on the first two of these three prongs of freedom policy in the first thesis of its current manifesto of 2012. The whole trident can then be found in the Andorra Manifesto of Liberal International of 2017.

Freedom policy means taking care of the practical validity, guarantee, balances and compatibility of formal right to freedom and usable life opportunities in the interplay of the three prongs. Optimising the balance of freedom over and over again is Sisyphean work for civilisation, a constant search, learning, balancing and peace project. In the economy, the Irish formula of the social market economy remains the mandate of such a freedom policy, to which not only the ordoliberal tradition but also opportunity policy in the labour market for entry, advancement and exit as well as the cultivation of corporate responsibility and social partnership contribute.

---

11 Möllers, Christoph: Freiheitsgrade. Elemente einer liberalen politischen Mechanik. Berlin: Suhrkamp 2020.
12 C.f. Kolev Stefan: Poison cupboard or treasure chest? Why each generation needs its own neoliberalism, in this volume.

Freedom policy as democracy policy

However, freedom policy must first and foremost apply to the political space in which we can make economic policy (and policy in general) in the first place. In other words, the open processes of searching, learning and shaping democracy. Freedom policy must always be democracy policy, and democracy policy should always be freedom policy: the concern for institutions, procedures, publics, associations, culture and personnel of free search, learning and shaping processes. Democracy is then freedom to participate, a common practice of globally effective self-execution. And liberal democratic politics in this sense would be the meta-political practice of shaping the conditions of a liberal democracy as a form of rule, government and life.[13]

Putin's frontal assault on Ukraine and on the best hopes of Europe's liberal democracies may now come as a vitalising shock. We will probably start by talking about "defensible democracy", which essentially means a domestic, security and legal policy agenda of defending democracy as a form of rule. But hopefully we will also quickly discuss strengthening a diverse, vibrant, capable and learning democracy as a form of government and life. And we should thus finally build up the policy field of "democracy policy", which goes back to a proposal by the liberal Hildegard Hamm-Brücher.[14]

After all, the concept of "democracy policy" is already in the coalition agreement of the German "traffic light" government. It includes comprehensive reforms of electoral law, a strengthening of parliament and its consultation with citizens, and the strengthening of democratic governance through planning law with participatory procedures. The participation competence of the administration is to be increased, a Democracy Promotion Act is to promote social cohesion and prevent extremism, a new national engagement strategy is to be created, civic infrastructures are to be renewed, migrants, children and young people are to be better involved and historical-political educational work is to be expanded. And much more.[15]

---

13 Gohl, Christopher: »Agenda zwischen Ambition und Abseits? Zur Demokratiepolitik der Ampel-Koalition.«, in: Forschungsjournal Soziale Bewegungen, 35: 1–2 (2022), S. 82-123.

14 Hamm-Brücher, Hildegard: Rede beim Stuttgarter Stiftungstag, Unveröffentlichtes Dokument, Theodor-Heuss-Stiftung 1998.

15 Gohl, Christopher: Agenda zwischen Ambition und Abseits? Zur Demokratiepolitik der Ampel-Koalition. In: Forschungsjournal Soziale Bewegungen 35/1 2022.

Unfortunately, however, these measures are completely scattered in the coalition agreement. Unfortunately, there is no central committee that could focus democracy policy as a forum for understanding and driver of change. And unfortunately, the coalition agreement is silent both on the guiding principle of a liberal democracy and on what is perhaps the greatest democratic challenge of the young decade, namely to transform the disruptive upheavals of the socio-ecological-economic transformation into peaceful awakenings. President Steinmeier elaborated on this challenge in his speech on his re-election on 13 February 2022. If democratic governance does not succeed here, our liberal democracy is in danger of perishing in the bondage of intensified distribution struggles, ecological disaster and increasing polarisation.

Outlook: Liberal democracy as a learning democracy

A liberal democracy defended as a form of rule, better organised as a form of government, and deepened as a form of life offers us, I believe, emancipative opportunities for permanently self-effective, open-ended and transformative action. We should understand and shape liberal democracy as a learning democracy: as a decentralised experimental practice of dialogically responsible use of freedom. And we should do this by

- embedding the maximised self-determination of the many (free and equal in rights) individuals in forms of optimised co-determination and limited, representative and justifiable governmental power, which appears to some as foreign domination because it also includes the restriction of individual freedoms;
- civilising political power and rule with civil rights and procedural rules, but at the same time, in joint intelligent action, also gaining creative power and thus freedoms that we do not have on our own;
- using the diverse and public use of reason to clarify moral sentiments and to inform and assure the quality of well-informed, wise decisions;
- critically scrutinising and adapting informal as well as legal norms of liberal coexistence again and again;
- in doing so, on the one hand, reasonably exploring and changing the conditions, entitlements and rights to better life chances of more people in the piecemeal meliorism of public critique and correction; and

- in doing so, on the other hand, making visible, negotiating and controlling the risks and paradoxes of the use of freedom for the continued existence of liberal societies.

Just as the social market economy emerged as a third way between unregulated capitalism and planned socialism, learning democracy would be a third way between smart technocratic elite rule and authoritarian populist mass dumbing down. Like fair competition in the social market economy, open dialogue would be a form of civil, productive and shared exercise of freedom. If we programme a modern, digitally networked democracy as an intelligent game of "freedom as method", we could transform the manifold pressures on liberal democracies into a push for progress. In the end, there is no capacity for peace without the capacity for dialogue, no capacity for dialogue without the capacity to learn – and no capacity to learn without the opportunities and protection of freedom.

A Civil Right to Further Education

Ralf Fücks and Rainald Manthe

Our world is changing at a rapid pace. What seemed secure yesterday can change tomorrow. In Western societies, there is a growing sense of insecurity that is also affecting the middle classes. Part of the population is reacting with aversion to the new. A majority is more pessimistic than confident about the future. This is the ground for authoritarian, nationalistic and xenophobic currents. They promise security by retreating into the national wagon fortress, by sealing themselves off from international competition and from the immigration of foreigners. Identitarian movements of folk or religious provenance are on the rise. The protests against Covid restrictions were the driving force behind a new system opposition.

Societies need security in times of change

There are many signs of growing social and cultural polarisation in Western societies. In times of rapid change, there is also growing insecurity among broad sections of society. Liberal democracies must take the conservative need for security seriously, without promising a continuation of the status quo. We cannot shield ourselves from the great changes of our time, but must embrace them as a *task of shaping the future.*

The guiding principle of democratic politics must not be security through isolation, but security in change or *through* change. This means more than mere adaptation to supposed constraints. If global competition, technological upheavals or the mass immigration of people from other parts of the world are experienced as mere natural phenomena that befall us, this destroys the legitimacy of liberal democracies.[1]

Shaping change means enabling people to keep pace with technical, social and cultural changes, to steer processes politically and to regulate markets. No one should be left unprotected in the face of the upheavals in the economy and society; everyone has the right to solidarity and participation.

At the same time, it is crucial to counteract the division of our societies into winners and losers of technological, cultural and ecological change. It undermines liberal democracy's promise of equal freedom for all. When growing insecurity meets growing inequality, the result is an explosive mix. Politics must create opportunities for all to shape their own lives – whatever shape they choose.

The world of work is changing

Work is central to the lives of many people. It provides income and esteem, gives meaning, creates value and enables self-realisation. The world of work is at the centre of economic and technological structural change. This process will accelerate in the coming years. Digitisation is leading to massive upheavals in the labour market. Various studies estimate that 43 per cent of today's jobs are at risk and 18 million new jobs will be created in Germany. There is a second megatrend: climate change is forcing the ecological transformation of the economy and society. The energy sector is changing from the ground up, the automotive industry is in upheaval, and new job profiles are emerging. Unexpected impacts such as the coronavirus pandemic or geopolitical crises reinforce the basic feeling of an uncertain future. As a result, the global economy changes abruptly, production is relocated back to Europe, and workers in new fields are urgently sought.

Education and further training are central to giving people security in the times of change: they enable individuals to keep pace with rapid changes and take control of their lives. Education must prepare people to deal with change confidently; continuing education can cushion breaks in professional biographies and open up new perspectives.

---

1   Center for Liberal Modernity: Security in Times of Change. Press Release, May 2019. https://libmod.de/en/report-security-in-times-of-change/

In order to cope with the structural change that is heading our way and to give as many people as possible the opportunity for professional development, we need continuing education on a large scale. But the sector is confusing, and the funding instruments are as fragmented as they are bureaucratic.

From educational leave to qualifications for job-seekers, from job-specific or company programmes to educational grants for adults and, in the new coalition agreement, the "Opportunities student financing", there are many special regulations and even more ideas for financing continuing education – and yet none that responds adequately to the structural changes in society. The fragmentation of access rules also means that continuing education cannot be used as a targeted instrument for tackling future challenges. Even if one would like to invest broadly, the instruments are simply lacking.

Continuing education is already a lived practice for many people. Over the course of the year, around half of the working population takes part in courses, training and seminars. A large proportion of this is accounted for by in-company continuing education, and only a small proportion by educational measures that primarily follow personal inclinations and interests. However, it is precisely this part that is becoming increasingly important in the context of structural change. Another important finding is that continuing education is unevenly distributed. It is primarily the domain of more highly qualified employees in more secure occupations and larger companies. There are also major regional differences, as the Bertelsmann Foundation shows in its "Continuing Education Atlas".[2] Up to now, more than two-thirds of continuing education has been financed privately, i.e. by companies and private individuals. The state provides only a small proportion of the funding.

A civil right to further education

For all these reasons, we need a different kind of funding for continuing education. One that makes it easier for a greater number of people to develop professionally and that gives them the chance to do something completely different again in their lives.

---

2   Bertelsmann Stiftung (Ed.): Deutscher Weiterbildungsatlas. Teilnahme und Angebot in Kreisen und kreisfreien Städten, 2018.

We therefore propose a basic education income.[3] It realises a right to further education and underpins it with an entitlement to time off work and basic financial security.

The basic education income is tied to federally recognised continuing education. It can be drawn for up to 36 months in the course of working life. Those interested receive qualified further training advice. The important thing is that they are free to decide what they use the basic income for. Although they have to take advantage of the counselling, they are not bound by its outcome. This strengthens the degrees of freedom, but does not let them walk blindly through the multitude of offers.

The only important thing is that the qualifications must be professionally useful. The training measure must last at least 3 months at a time, also to keep administrative costs within reasonable limits. Accompanying measures such as nationwide certification improve the comparability of continuing education offerings. At the same time, it is important to continuously improve the quality of the offerings, for example through appropriate investments in structure and, above all, personnel.

Recipients of the basic education income receive a flat rate of 1,200 euros per month. In addition, there are supplementary allowances for children or special impairments. Course costs, material and travel costs are covered and social security contributions continue to be paid during the period of entitlement. This ensures that people are not worse off later in terms of their pension than they would have been without further training.

Nevertheless, the bottom line for many will be that they will be in a worse position for a short time, so that they will have to fall back on their savings or employer subsidies to secure their standard of living. Continuing education is also an investment in one's future that pays off for the vast majority. Low-income earners, on the other hand, will hardly have less money than before – which could increase their willingness to undergo further training. The easy accessibility of the instrument should reduce further hurdles.[4]

---

3 C.f. Zentrum Liberale Moderne (Ed.): Das Bildungsgrundeinkommen. Vorschlag für eine neue Weiterbildungsfinanzierung, 2021.

4 C.f. Machbarkeitsstudie im Auftrag von Bertelsmann-Stiftung und Zentrum Liberale Moderne: Prognos: Wege zu einem zukunftsfähigen Weiterbildungssystem. Die Umsetzung eines Bildungsgrundeinkommens, Berlin 2022.

Higher tax revenues would partially refinance basic education income

The basic education income is financed from tax revenues. This is appropriate given the immense importance of continuing education in managing structural change and its positive effects on productivity and employment. A good part of the expenditure will be refinanced over time through higher tax revenues or lower unemployment expenses.

A basic education income will enable a significantly larger number of people to develop or reorient themselves professionally. In doing so, they are neither subject to the often small-scale programmes nor bound to the preferences of their employer. They are free to decide what direction they want to give their lives. With its low access threshold and basic financial security, the basic education income can motivate more people to continue their education.

Everyone should be able to take their life into their own hands

The basic education income has great emancipatory potential. It offers the possibility of greater self-determination in a world of rapid change. A financially secured right to further education is not only an investment in "human capital". It strengthens the ability to take one's life into one's own hands and thus also confidence in liberal democracy. At the international level, a basic education income could, for example, be financed through funds for continuing education if countries lack the financial resources to do this themselves.

The basic education income is an example of how politics can ensure security in times of rapid change. It gives people time, money and guidance to develop on their own. It is easy to understand and access, it enables self-determined decisions and mediates between the needs for security and freedom.

Authors

Alexandra Borchardt is a journalist, book author, lecturer and consultant. She is co-director of the Journalism Innovators Program at the Hamburg Media School, Honorary Professor for Leadership and Digitization at the TUM School of Management at the Technical University of Munich, and Senior Research Associate at the Reuters Institute for the Study of Journalism at the University of Oxford.

Sabine A. Döring is State Secretary in the Federal Ministry of Education and Research. She is also Professor of Philosophy with a focus on Practical Philosophy at the University of Tübingen. She regularly publishes essays on her research interests. She is currently working on a book about freedom and the common good.

Gabriel Felbermayr is director of the Austrian Institute of Economic Research (WIFO) in Vienna and a professor at the Vienna University of Economics and Business (WU. Previously, he was president of the Kiel Institute for the World Economy. He is a member of the Scientific Advisory Board of the German Federal Ministry of Economics and Energy, Chairman of the Statistics Council of Statistics Austria, and co-editor of the "European Economic Review". His main research interests are international trade theory and policy, labor market research and European economic integration.

Ralf Fücks is founder and managing partner of the Center for Liberal Modernity in Berlin. He has been Chairman of the Heinrich Böll Foundation for 21 years, where he was responsible for the foundation's domestic work as well as for foreign and security policy, Europe and North America. He publishes in

German and international media on issues of sustainable development, political strategy and international politics.

Christopher Gohl is a political scientist at the Global Ethic Institute in Tübingen since 2012. He was member of the Bundestag for the Free Democratic Party (FDP) and still is head of the Freedom and Ethics Commission for the party's federal executive. He contributed to the FDP's current manifesto and to the Andorra Manifesto of the Liberal International. Gohl regularly publishes on fundamental programmatic issues of liberalism and the development of democracy.

Rainer Hank is a publicist and columnist and headed the economics and finance editorial department of the Frankfurter Allgemeine Sonntags-zeitung. He received the Karl Hermann Flach Prize, is member of the jury for the Ludwig Erhard Prize for Economic Journalism, and member of the Wilhelm Röpke Institute.

Karen Horn teaches economic history of ideas and economic journalism at the University of Erfurt. She is also a publicist and renowned economic journalist. She writes for the Neue Zürcher Zeitung and the Frankfurter Allgemeine Zeitung, among others. Karen Horn is co-initiator and coordinator of the international academic network "NOUS".

Stefan Kolev is professor of economic policy at the West Saxon University of Applied Sciences in Zwickau and head of the Ludwig-Erhard-Forum. He is deputy chairman of the Wilhelm Röpke Institute, member of the advisory board of the Aktionsgemeinschaft Soziale Marktwirtschaft, and a research fellow at the Hamburg Institute of International Economics. In 2015, he co-founded international academic network "NOUS".

Sabine Leutheusser-Schnarrenberger is a former Federal Minister of Justice and Deputy Chairwoman of the Friedrich Naumann Foundation for Freedom. She is also the first antisemitism commissioner of the state of North Rhine-Westphalia and, since 2019, a member of the Bavarian Constitutional Court. She regularly publishes on topics at the intersection of law and democracy.

Amichai Magen is a lecturer and director of the Democratic Resilience and Development Program at the Lauder School of Government, Diplomacy and

Strategy, at the Interdisciplinary Center (IDC), Herzliya, Israel, and chair of the Governance & Political Violence Program at the Institute for Counter-Terrorism (ICT) in Herzliya. He researches and publishes on state sovereignty, democracy, rule of law, governance in spaces of limited statehood, and political violence.

Rainald Manthe is a sociologist, author, and program director for Liberal Democracy at the Center for Liberal Modernity. He has a PhD in sociology on the transnational encounters of social movements and publishes regularly on questions of the development of democracy.

Christoph Möllers is Professor of Public Law and Philosophy of Law at the Humboldt University of Berlin and Permanent Fellow at the Institute for Advanced Study in Berlin. His research focuses on the fields of German, European and comparative constitutional law, democratic theory and the theory of social norms. He was the winner of the DFG (German Research Foundation) Gotthold Wilhelm Leibniz Prize in 2016.

Jan-Werner Müller teaches political theory and the history of ideas at Princeton University. His latest book "Democracy Rules" was published in 2021 with Macmillan USA.

Jacques Rupnik is Professor at CERI-Sciences Po in Paris and Guest Professor at College of Europe in Bruges. He is an expert in East- and Central European History and European Integration.

Cornelia Schu holds a doctorate in German studies and has many years of experience at the interfaces of science, politics and the foundation sector. Since 2014, she has managed the affairs of the Sachverständigenrat für Integration und Migration gGmbH [previously: Sachverstän-digenrat deutscher Stiftungen für Integration und Migration GmbH]. She gained broad expertise in integration policy as head of the thematic focus on integration at the Mercator Foundation.

Daniela Schwarzer heads the Open Society Foundations in Europe and Eurasia. Previously, she was director of the German Council on Foreign Relations. She is an honorary professor at Freie Universität Berlin. Her most recent book,

"Final Call – How Europe Can Hold Its Own Between China and the United States," was published by Campus Verlag.

Achim Wambach has been President of ZEW – Leibniz Centre for European Economic Research and Professor of Economics at the University of Mannheim since 2016. He was a member of the Monopolies Commission from 2014 to June 2022 and its chairman from 2016 to 2020. He is a member of the Scientific Advisory Board of the German Federal Ministry of Economics, which he chaired from 2012–2015. In 2018–2019, he was co-chair of the Commission "Competition Law 4.0" of the Federal Ministry of Economics. In his research, Achim Wambach deals, among other things, with issues of competition policy and market design.

Karolina Wigura is a historian, sociologist, and political editor of Kultural Liberalna, Poland's leading online political and cultural weekly. She is a lecturer at the Institute of Sociology at the University of Warsaw and works on 20th century political philosophy, emotions in politics, and the sociology and ethics of memory.

Michael Zürn is Professor of International Relations at Freie Universität Berlin and Director of the Department of Global Governance at the Berlin Social Science Center. Together with Tanja Börzel, he is the spokesperson for the Cluster of Excellence "Contestations of the Liberal Script (SCRIPTS)".

[transcript]

PUBLISHING. KNOWLEDGE. TOGETHER.

transcript publishing stands for a multilingual transdisciplinary programme in the social sciences and humanities. Showcasing the latest academic research in various fields and providing cutting-edge diagnoses on current affairs and future perspectives, we pride ourselves in the promotion of modern educational media beyond traditional print and e-publishing. We facilitate digital and open publication formats that can be tailored to the specific needs of our publication partners.

OUR SERVICES INCLUDE

- partnership-based publishing models
- Open Access publishing
- innovative digital formats: HTML, Living Handbooks, and more
- sustainable digital publishing with XML
- digital educational media
- diverse social media linking of all our publications

Visit us online: www.transcript-publishing.com

Find our latest catalogue at www.transcript-publishing.com/newbookspdf